THE Tech
Contracts
POCKET GUIDE

THE Tech Contracts

POCKET GUIDE

Software and Services Agreements for
Salespeople, Contract Managers,

Business Developers, and Lawyers

David W. Tollen, Esq.

iUniverse, Inc.
New York Lincoln Shanghai

The Tech Contracts Pocket Guide
Software and Services Agreements for Salespeople, Contract Managers, Business
Developers, and Lawyers

Copyright © 2006 by David W. Tollen

iUniverse books may be ordered through booksellers or by contacting:

iUniverse
2021 Pine Lake Road, Suite 100
Lincoln, NE 68512
www.iuniverse.com
1-800-Authors (1-800-288-4677)

ISBN-13: 978-0-595-40217-5 (pbk)
ISBN-13: 978-0-595-84593-4 (ebk)
ISBN-10: 0-595-40217-8 (pbk)
ISBN-10: 0-595-84593-2 (ebk)

Printed in the United States of America

Special thanks to Christopher B. Conner, Frederick Gault Jr., Michael F. Kelleher, and Robert W. Tollen. Thanks also to Paul Ambrosio, Jay Botelho, Lee Bruno, Ralph Chandler, Matteo Daste, Gary S. Davis, R. Oak Dowling, Ron Epstein, Sean M. Fitzgerald, Jennifer Hanley, Nels Johnson, Kathy O'Sullivan, Martin Plack, Robert A. Preskill, Colin Rule, Ken Stratton, Larry Townsend, Cydney A. Tune, and Amy Ward.

Please also visit this book's website:

www.TechContracts.net

CONTENTS

INTRODUCTION

This book will help you negotiate, write, and understand information technology contracts. Specifically, it will help you with software licenses and other software transfers, as well as technology services agreements. It focuses on business deals, rather than consumer contracts.

This book is for both lawyers and non-lawyers. The text doesn't use any technical jargon—any "legalese," "engineerese," or "programmerese." It's written in simple English, like a good contract.

You can use this book as a training manual or as a reference guide, or both. If you're training, read this book cover-to-cover. It provides an overview of the key technology contracting concepts. A cover-to-cover review will be particularly useful if you're new to the field.

If you need a reference guide, on the other hand, you can pick and choose the sections to read. If you're negotiating a contract, or reading or writing one, look up the various clauses to learn what they mean and what's at stake. You can also use this book as a source of sample contract language. Each listing includes one or more example clauses. And the appendix, starting on page 125, contains a full-length contract form. (Currently, you can download that form, free of charge, at this book's website: www.TechContracts.net.) Finally, you can use this book—particularly the table of contents—as a check-list for clauses to consider.

This book can't replace a lawyer—or a colleague with more IT contracts experience, if you are a lawyer. But it can help you understand your lawyer—or colleague. And whether you have legal help or not, the better you understand your contracts, the more effective you will be.

I'm a technology lawyer, and this book grew out of a seminar I teach, for both attorneys and non-attorneys. At the end of the program, students would often ask where they can learn more—if there's a good book on software and services contracts. Most of the books I knew were massive tomes on intellectual property or contract law. They're written for lawyers only, and their more practical lessons are spread across hundreds or thousands of pages. I had learned much of my trade on the job, rather than from a book. I've served as a technology lawyer with a global firm, as general counsel for a publicly traded software company, and as vice president of business development for an Internet start-up. I now practice through my own technology-focused law firm in San Francisco. The material for my seminar came from the contracts I've negotiated and written in those positions. I'd never seen a really concise outline of the issues, except my seminar agendas and instructor's notes (the latter only half legible, even to me). So I wrote this book.

*   *   *   *

The rest of this introduction provides more detail about the types of contracts this book covers. It also teaches three lessons about contracting in general. Finally, it explains the structure of a contract and of this book, and it offers a few explanations that will help you get the most out of your reading.

Software, Services, and IT

This book covers (1) software contracts, (2) information technology services contracts, and (3) combination contracts, which include both software and services. The text calls the parties to all these agreements the "provider" and the "recipient."

Software contracts include end-user licenses, assignments, work-for-hire agreements, and distribution agreements (including value-added reseller and original equipment manufacturer licenses). In all of these deals, the provider transfers intellectual property ("IP") rights to the recipient. Those rights might be limited, like the right to copy or distribute software. Or the recipient might receive all IP rights and become the software's new owner.

Services contracts call on the provider to *help* the recipient, rather than to provide software or IP. The provider is going to *do* something. In the information technology ("IT") industry, that help generally has something to do with software and computers. IT services include data management, network management, technology maintenance, system integration, and integrated circuit design, to name just a few. IT also includes the computer-related activities of both the Internet and the telecommunications industry. So IT services include website development and provision of Internet access.

Finally, in a combination contract, the provider agrees to provide both software and services. Computer programming contracts, for instance, usually call on the provider to write software, a service, and to transfer IP rights in that software. Technology integration agreements often work the same way: the provider licenses or sells software to the recipient, and also provides a service by integrating all those applications into a computer system. A combination contract works like two contracts in one. It needs terms appropriate for both software and services.

Three Lessons about Contracting

1. *Good fences make good neighbors.*

Why do we sign contracts? It's not because we want to win a lawsuit later. It's not because we don't trust each other. It's not even because we're afraid lawyers will stir up trouble if they're not kept busy.

We sign contracts because good fences make good neighbors.

The best way to avoid arguments in a business relationship is to write down the parties' expectations ahead of time. That list becomes a boundary-marker—like a fence between neighboring yards—explaining who is responsible for what. If the parties disagree, they can look at the list for guidance. Usually, that list becomes a contract.

In other words, contracts *prevent* disputes—at least, good ones do. They prevent lawsuits.

Even if the parties never look back at the contract once it's signed, it still has probably played a vital role. When people put their business expectations on paper, they often find those expectations don't match. Just the act of negotiating a written[1] contract will uncover many mismatched expectations. The parties can address them before starting work.

Yes, it is true that we sometimes fight over contracts in lawsuits. And yes, in interpreting a contract, we often talk about what a judge would say it means. But that's only because courts have the ultimate say, if the parties can't agree. Job number one for the contract is to keep the parties out of court.

2. *There is no such thing as "legalese" or "technicalese."*

You may feel uncomfortable with contracts because of the unfamiliar language they use. Don't be intimidated. You can understand most contracts.

There really is no such thing as legalese. American contracts are written in English (or Spanish or Vietnamese or whatever language the parties speak). But contracts do sometimes use special shorthand—terms lawyers have developed to save time. And some IT contracts use "technical shorthand." Finally, contracts sometimes use formal, stilted language with long run-on sentences. Don't let shorthand or stilted language bother you.

---

1   Many contracts can be oral rather than written, but some can't. And oral contracts have serious disadvantages. Without a clear recording of the terms, the parties have to rely on memories, so the contract won't serve as much of a roadmap. And oral contracts usually cover only high-level issues, leaving doubt about whether the parties actually agree on vital details.

If you run into an unfamiliar term in a contract—unfamiliar shorthand—don't worry. Look it up. If it's legal shorthand, you can probably find the definition in a standard dictionary, or online, or in *Black's Law Dictionary*,[2] found in many libraries. Or, better yet, ask a lawyer. Treat technical terms the same way. Look them up in a dictionary or technical manual or online. Or ask someone with the right expertise.

Once you understand a term, feel free to use it in your own contracts. But you should also feel free *not* to use it. Shorthand is optional. If you do use shorthand, be sure the contract defines each technical term. Definitions can vary for IT terms like "RGB" and "bot,"[3] so the contract needs an agreed definition, unless there really can't be any doubt. (See *The Structure of a Contract and of this Book*, on page 5, for more on defined terms.) Legal terms, on the other hand, often have widely-accepted definitions, so you usually don't need to define them in the contract.

As for long sentences, just take a deep breath and read slowly. The same goes for formal language. There really is no reason to use terms like "heretofore" and "ipso facto." That sort of language often appears in form contracts from the olden days, when formal writing was more popular. It does crop up in modern contracts—often because someone wants to show off a big vocabulary. Be suitably impressed. Then take out your dictionary if necessary, and figure out what each sentence says. And avoid terms like that in your own writing.

3. *Leverage is everything; "fairness" is nothing.*

A lot of people who negotiate contracts get tied up in knots over what is *fair*. They feel outraged if they're "forced" to sign an "unfair" contract. That's a bad way to look at contracts. You will do better if you think about *leverage*, not fairness.

In general, no one *has* to sign a contract. So if you do agree to terms you dislike, terms that seem "unfair," you probably are getting something worthwhile. Obviously, you're not getting as much as you wanted, but you wouldn't have agreed if the exchange wasn't better than nothing—better than not doing business at all. So long as no one's pointing a gun at your head (or otherwise forcing you through illegal "duress"), whatever terms you accept are probably fair.[4]

---

2   From the West Publishing Company.

3   "RGB": red-green-blue, a term used for computer screen technology. "Bot": a software program that mimics human behavior, in that it's automated, (short for "robot").

4   OK, that's not entirely true, at least as far as the law is concerned. There are some terms courts won't enforce because they're "opposed to public policy."

So if considerations of fairness *aren't* decisive, how do the parties resolve differences of opinion during negotiations? What guides the arguing and negotiating, and the eventual compromise or knuckling-under that leads to a contract? The principle in question is *leverage*.

If you need the deal more than the other party, you will probably give more. And visa-versa. It's that simple. Don't get upset about it, and when you're in the power position, don't take advantage of it too much. You never know when positions will reverse.

The Structure of a Contract and of this Book

Software and services contract terms fall into three groups: transactional clauses, general clauses, and supporting clauses. This book is organized the same way.

The transactional clauses express the deal's central terms. There, the provider grants a license or other rights to software, or promises to provide services—or both. The recipient, on the other hand, promises to pay. This book addresses transactional clauses in Part I, starting on page 11.

The general clauses account for most of the rest of the contract. They cover everything not addressed in the transactional clauses or the supporting clauses. This book addresses general clauses in Part II, starting on page 52.

Supporting clauses cover the theoretically non-controversial mechanics of a deal: terms on independent contractor status, contract construction, choice of law, etc. IT industry professionals call many of these clauses "boilerplate" and place them at the end of a contract. This book addresses supporting clauses in Part III, on page 116.

Most contracts start with two sets of supporting clauses: the introduction and recitals and the definitions.[5] From there on, you should organize your clauses the way they're listed above: transactional clauses, then general clauses, then the remaining supporting clauses. That makes agreements easy to understand. Unfortunately though, you will probably find contracts with the clauses jumbled together, in no particular order.

---

5   See *Introduction and Recitals*, Section III.A, on page 117; and *Definitions*, Section III.B, on page 117.

Using This Book

The following four brief explanations will help you get the most out of this book.

First, "one size fits all" rarely works for contracts. Good contracts are customized. So look at this book as a source of *general* lessons to be applied thoughtfully to each deal. Your deal probably raises unique issues no book could cover in advance. "We don't have an office near Albuquerque, so services there will be delayed." "We can't promise the software will work on a Linux system because we've never tested it." "Our CEO gets hives if we pay more than twenty percent in advance." This book offers building blocks for a contract addressing issues like those, but the customizations are up to you.

Bear that in mind as you review the example clauses. This book is full of sample contract language, mostly in gray-colored *clause boxes*. If you put one of those clauses into your contract, you will probably need to tweak it. To take a simple example, imagine you're looking for a clause requiring that tech services providers have enough experience. You turn to this book's section on service provider experience and find an example clause: "All Provider's assigned staff-members will have five (5) or more years' full-time experience with computer programming." The problem is, your contract calls for tech support, not programming, and you don't really need five years' experience. You've got to tweak the sample clause: "All Provider's assigned staff-members will have *one (1) or more year* of full-time experience *supporting or maintaining CrashProne, Inc. computer systems.*" And if the sample clause fits your deal only loosely, you've got to tweak it more creatively. The sample is just a starting point.[6]

Second, this book addresses American law. That means it may not be useful for foreign contracts. Within the U.S., the fifty states have similar contract laws, and federal law governs some of the issues discussed here. But you should be aware that state laws do vary. Some lessons here apply better to one state than another. That's one of the reasons you should consider help from an experienced lawyer.

Third, like most contracts, the examples in this book use defined terms. When a contract creates a concept and uses it more than once, it usually defines it. For instance, a contract might list the provider's services in section 2, then mention them over and over in other sections. Rather than listing the services repeatedly, the contract defines the list as the "Services." Whenever the

---

6   The example clauses use made-up names (e.g., "Nemesis Corporation," "Protecto Systems"). Obviously, you should replace those with real world names from your deal.

contract refers to "the Services" with a capital "S," it means the whole list. This book's sample clauses work the same way: capitalized words that aren't proper names represent defined terms (e.g., "Software," "Effective Date," "Statement of Work," this "Agreement"). So do sets of initials in all caps, like "NDA" (nondisclosure agreement). Often, the sample clause won't supply the definition. That's because, in a real contract, that term would be defined in another section. Obviously, in your contracts, you should provide definitions somewhere for all such terms. For more on defined terms, see *Definitions*, Section III.B, on page 117.[7]

Fourth and finally, two of the sample clauses' defined terms are "Provider" and "Recipient." As noted above, the text refers to the contracting parties the same way. Don't be confused if contracts you've seen use other names. "Provider" stands in for "Licensor," "Vendor," "Seller," and "Consultant," among others. And "Recipient" stands in for "Licensee," "Customer," "Buyer," and "Client." This book favors "Provider" and "Recipient" because they're generic. But the text does occasionally use party names like "Distributor" where necessary to avoid confusion.

---

7   Some contracts mark defined terms with all caps instead of initial caps: e.g., "SOFTWARE."

The Clauses

I. Transactional Clauses

The transactional clauses are the key terms in most technology contracts. They provide for the fundamental transaction: the exchange of software or services for money or other consideration.

Most software and services contracts include two of the clauses described in this part: (1) a transfer or sale of software rights or services (Sections I.A through I.F) and (2) a promise of payment (Section I.G). But combination contracts—agreements with multiple transactions—may include several transactional clauses.

A. Standard End-User Software License

A copyright license grants the recipient rights to copy software or to exploit it in other ways. It leaves ownership with the provider. A license works like a rental agreement. The provider/landlord still owns the house, but the recipient/tenant gets to use it.

This section looks at standard end-user licenses. It doesn't go far into the mechanics of copyright licensing, because that kind of knowledge isn't always necessary to understand a standard license. But if you want a deeper understanding of licensing, or if your license isn't standard, see *Software Licenses in General*, Section I.C, on page 20.

In a standard end-user license, the recipient will run the software for internal business purposes, like word processing, data management, etc. The recipient won't share the software with third parties: it won't rent software out to its own customers, for instance. Therefore, the contract doesn't need a lot of detail about *how* the recipient can run the software.

Before turning to the terms of an end-user license, ask yourself: *what* is being licensed? The contract should clearly define the "Software" or "Licensed Product"—in the license clause itself, or in a separate definitions section. In a standard license, it's usually enough to give the software's name and version number, and specify object code: "'Software' refers to Provider's GlitchMaster software application, version 3.0, in object code format."[1] But if the software has multiple modules or libraries or whatever, or if you see any chance of dispute about what's included, list the necessary elements—and involve someone

---

1   "Object code" generally refers to code a computer can read. It's also sometimes called "machine-readable code." Object code is contrasted with "source code": code a human programmer can read, which gets "compiled" or translated into object code. Those are simplified definitions though, so consider doing some research or getting technical help if you need to understand code types better.

with a technical background if necessary. "'Licensed Product' refers to Provider's *VacuumEx for the PC* software application, version 4.05, in object code format, including the following modules: VacuumManager, Client Controller, and Rug Stopwatch." You might also specify the platform: Windows, Macintosh, Linux, etc. Finally, if the recipient needs to reproduce user manuals and other documentation, the definition should include them: "The Licensed Product includes Provider's standard user manuals and other documentation for such software."[2]

1. End-User Rights

A license is a grant of rights. A standard end-user license grants the right to "reproduce" software, the right to "use" it, or both.[3]

> *Standard End-User Rights*
>
> Provider hereby grants Recipient a non-exclusive, non-transferable license to reproduce thirty (30) copies of the Licensed Product. Recipient may use the Licensed Product for internal business purposes only. Provider retains full title to and ownership of the Licensed Product.
>
> —
>
> Provider hereby grants Recipient a non-exclusive license to reproduce and use the Software as necessary for Recipient's internal business purposes. The rights granted in this Section 2 are not extended to any parent, subsidiary, or affiliate of Recipient. This Agreement grants recipient no title to or ownership of the Software.

The license should specify the number of copies the recipient can make and use (even if that's "1"). The clearest way is to list a number, as in the first example in the clause box above. Sometimes, however, the provider isn't concerned with the number of copies, and the parties agree on an "enterprise license," as in the second example above. A provider should only grant an enterprise

---

2   For more on documentation, see *Documentation*, Section II.L, on page 96.

3   IP lawyers debate the value of "use" rights in copyright licenses, but they're fine for purposes of this Section. If you'd like to know more about the debate, see *Software Licenses in General, Copyright License Rights*, Subsection I.C.1, discussion of *Use (a pseudo-right)* on page 24.

licenses if it knows the size of the recipient's business and knows it won't expand much—or if the fees are high enough to cover any likely expansion. Also, providers—particularly of enterprise licenses—should consider restricting the software to the recipient itself and forbidding use by subsidiaries, parent companies, and other affiliates. Again, see the second example.

A standard end-user license should also specify that the recipient can use the software only for "internal business purposes," as in both examples in the clause box above.

Finally, every license should confirm that the recipient receives no ownership rights. See both examples in the clause box.

2. End-User Restrictions

A key restriction in any end-user license is time: when do the recipient's rights expire? If the license clause says nothing on the subject, the rights expire when the contract terminates.[4] The clause can also specify its own date: "Provider hereby grants Recipient, during the two (2) years following the Effective Date, a license to…."

End-user licenses generally limit the recipient's use of software in other ways.

Standard End-User Restrictions

Recipient receives no rights to the Software other than those specifically granted in this Section 2. Without limiting the generality of the foregoing,[5] Recipient will not: (a) modify, create derivative works from, distribute, publicly display, publicly perform, or sublicense the Software; (b) use the Software for service bureau or time-sharing purposes or in any other way allow third parties to exploit the Software; or (c) reverse engineer, decompile, disassemble, or otherwise attempt to derive any of the Software's source code.

---

4   See *Term and Termination*, Section II.R, on page 110.

5   "Without limiting the generality of the foregoing" is a quick way to say: "The last sentence gave the general rule. This sentence gives examples of that rule in action, but they're not the only examples possible." In the clause above, the phrase means the recipient only gets the rights specified. The fact that the next sentence lists certain rights withheld doesn't mean the recipient gets all other rights *not* specifically withheld.

The provider should make sure the recipient receives only those rights specifically granted, as in the example in the clause box above.

An end-user license should also list certain rights *not* granted. Copyright law grants several exclusive rights to copyright owners. Providers should make sure the license doesn't grant any of these except the right to reproduce (along with the right to use, which isn't actually mentioned in the copyright statute). That's why the example in the clause box provides that the recipient can't exercise the other rights of copyright holders. It can't distribute, modify (create derivative works from), or publicly display or perform the software. The recipient also can't sublicense its rights to anyone else. Of course, if the clause is silent on restrictions, a court will probably consider the license limited to the rights specifically granted. But why take chances?

The provider should also clarify that the recipient gets no time-sharing or service bureau rights, or any other rights to share the software with third parties. "Time-sharing" means sharing an application with customers or other third parties: letting them use the software too. "Service bureau" usage involves another type of sharing: the recipient keeps the software, but it uses it to process third party data, instead of its own internal data. Either could cost the provider sales.

Finally, the provider should be sure the license forbids reverse engineering and any other attempt to derive source code from the software.[6]

---

6   See the footnote on page 12 for a definition of "source code."

B. Standard Distributor Software License

This section addresses licenses to distribute software. In these clauses, the provider authorizes a distributor to transfer copyrighted software to third parties—to customers. This section, therefore, talks about "distributors" rather than "recipients."

Like Section I.A, this section doesn't go far into the mechanics of copyright licensing. That kind of knowledge isn't always necessary to understand a standard distributor license. But if you want a deeper understanding of licensing, or if your license isn't standard, see *Software Licenses in General*, Section I.C, on page 20.

Before turning to the terms of a distributor license, ask: *what* is being licensed? The contract should clearly define the "Software" or "Licensed Product"—in the license clause itself or in a separate definitions section. It's usually enough to give the software's name and version number, and specify object code: "'Software' refers to Provider's CookieCruncher software application, version 6.02, in object code format." But if the software has multiple modules or libraries or whatever, and you see any chance of dispute about what's included, list the necessary elements—and involve someone with technical experience if needed. "'Licensed Product' refers to Provider's *RoboSurgeon for the PC* software application, version 2.0, in object code format, including the following modules: RemoteScalpel, Anesthesia-Alarm, and MalpracticManager." You might also want to specify the platform: Windows, Macintosh, Linux, etc. Finally, if the distributor needs to distribute user manuals or other documentation, the definition should include them: "The Licensed Product includes Provider's standard user guides and other documentation for such software."[1]

---

1   For definitions of "object code" and "source code," see the footnote on page 12. For more on documentation, see *Documentation*, Section II.L, on page 96.

1. Distribution Rights

Not surprisingly, a distribution license grants the right to distribute the software—to pass it around.

Standard Distributor Rights

Provider grants Distributor an exclusive license to distribute the Licensed Product to the public within the state of New York. Provider further grants Distributor a non-exclusive license to reproduce, use, perform, and display the Licensed Product within the continental United States, solely as necessary to market it. Provider retains full title to and ownership of the Licensed Product.

—

Subject to the royalty provisions of Section 4 and the other terms and conditions of this Agreement, Provider hereby grants Distributor a non-exclusive, worldwide license: (a) to distribute the Software to the public, solely as an embedded component of Distributor's Value-Added Product; (b) to reproduce, use, perform, and display the Software, solely for sales and marketing purposes in support of such distribution; (c) to sublicense to its customers the right to reproduce and use the Software; and (d) to sublicense to its sub-distributors the rights granted in (a) through (c) of this sentence. This Agreement grants Distributor no title to or ownership of the Software.

Distribution rights are often restricted to a territory, as in the first example in the clause box above. The distributor has no right to distribute outside the territory.

The right may be exclusive or non-exclusive. If it's exclusive, no one, not even the provider, has authority to distribute within the territory—or anywhere, if the license is world-wide.

Some distribution licenses include limited rights to reproduce, use, perform, or display the software, as in both examples in the clause box above. These rights help with marketing. Technically speaking, the clause should grant these rights, and you should include them in your distribution licenses. But sometimes it's fair to assume a distributor has reasonable marketing rights, even if they're not spelled out.

Value-added reseller ("VAR") licenses grant limited distribution rights. The distributor can only give the software out as a component of some larger application—often something the distributor itself sells. Imagine the provider makes databases and the distributor makes factory-management applications, which use databases. A VAR license lets the distributor distribute the provider's database *with* the distributor's application, giving end-user customers a complete package. But the distributor can't distribute the database as a stand-alone product. The second example in the clause box is a VAR license.

Original equipment manufacturer ("OEM") licenses grant the same basic rights as VAR licenses. Technically speaking, in an OEM licenses, the distributor's product is always equipment—hardware—while a VAR license may involve hardware or software. But many IT professionals use the terms interchangeably.

Some distribution licenses let the distributor sublicense its rights to its sub-distributors, as in the second example in the clause box. Providers should make sure the contract's payment clause requires royalties or other payments whether it's a distributor or sub-distributor that makes the sale.[2] Some clauses also let the distributor sublicense certain rights to customers. In the second example in the clause box, the distributor can grant its customers the right to reproduce and use the software. Few distribution licenses actually specify these rights, though. Most providers and distributors assume sublicensing rights are implied in the right to distribute—and that's usually a fair assumption.

Finally, every license should confirm that the distributor receives no ownership rights. See both examples in the clause box.

2. Distribution Restrictions

A key restriction in a distributor license is time: when do the distributor's rights expire? If the license clause says nothing on the subject—as in the example in the clause box below—they expire when the contract terminates.[3] The clause can also specify its own termination date: "Provider hereby grants Distributor, during the two (2) years following the Effective Date, a license to...."

License clauses often restrict distributors in other ways.

---

2   For payment clauses, see *Payment*, Section I.G, on page 49.
3   See *Term and Termination*, Section II.R, on page 110.

> ### *Standard Distributor Restrictions*
>
> Distributor receives no rights to the Software other than those specifically granted in this Section 2. Without limiting the generality of the foregoing,[4] Distributor will not reverse engineer, decompile, disassemble, or otherwise attempt to derive any of the Software's source code. Distributor will not distribute copies of the Software to any third party that does not first execute a written agreement with limits on use of the Software no less restrictive than those set forth in the preceding two sentences.

The provider should clarify that the distributor receives only the rights specifically granted. And it should forbid reverse engineering and any other attempt to derive source code from the software. See the example in the clause box above.

The provider has another party to worry about, besides the distributor. What will the distributor's *customer* do with the software? That's why the license clause should provide that the distributor will have its customers sign agreements that restrict their software use, as in the example in the clause box.

---

4   For an explanation of this phrase, see the footnote on page 14.

C. Software Licenses in General

Section I.A addresses standard end-user software licenses, while I.B addresses standard distribution licenses. This section provides a more thorough review of copyright licensing in general. It provides concepts you can use to customize licenses that don't fit those standard models. But the previous two sections do explain some key concepts. So before reviewing this section, read I.A if you're working on an end-user license, and I.B for a distributor license.

This section addresses two issues. Subsection 1 asks: *What rights does the provider grant?* Subsection 2 asks: *What is the scope of the license?* Are the rights exclusive, temporary, restricted, etc.—and if so how? Software licensing is a game of mix and match. You list the recipient's rights and then put them together with the appropriate scope terms.

Subsections 3 and 4 use all these lessons to show you an "unrestricted license" and an "open source license." An unrestricted license grants the recipient as many rights as possible without actually transferring ownership. Recipients who pay for software development sometimes want this sort of license. An open source license grants the whole world rights to software, though often with important restrictions in the scope terms. (If you're not interested in unrestricted or open-sources licenses, there's no reason to read Subsection 3 or 4.)

Always start by clearly defining the "Software" or "Licensed Product." For guidance on these definitions, see Section I.A on page 12 for end-user licenses, and I.B on page 16 for distributor licenses. Note that in technology development contracts, it's often impossible to identify all the software at the time the contract's drafted. There, the definition should read something like: "'Licensed Product' refers to all software to be created pursuant to this Agreement"—or "all software to be created pursuant to a Statement of Work."[1]

---

1   For statements of work, see *Promise of Professional Services, Multiple Statements of Work*, Subsection I.E.3, on page 43.
Footnote continued on next page.

1. Copyright License Rights

Software licenses are copyright licenses. Under U.S. federal law, the copyright owner has certain exclusive rights. In a license, the owner grants the recipient some of those rights.[2]

The license should list the rights granted. And for the provider's sake, the license should also list the rights that *are not* granted, to make sure there's no confusion. Finally, all licenses should confirm that the recipient receives no *ownership* interest.

Often, the most important terms of a software license are the scope terms, addressed in Subsection 2 below. But for now, let's look at rights without scope terms, or with very limited scope terms.

Copyright Licenses (with Limited or No Scope Terms)

Provider herby grants Distributor a license: (a) to modify the Software; (b) to reproduce the resulting derivative work (the "Derivative Work"); (c) to distribute the Derivative Work to the public; (d) to reproduce, use, and publicly display and perform the Derivative Work as reasonably necessary for marketing purposes; (e) to sublicense to its customers the rights to reproduce and use the Derivative Work; and (f) to sublicense to its distributors the rights granted in Subsections (b) through (e) above. Provider retains full title to and ownership of the Software.

As Sections I.A and I.B explain, you should usually specify object code in the definition of "Software." But if the contract calls for creation of the Software, a definition limited to object code wouldn't make sense, since the provider starts by writing *source code*. In those cases, the definition doesn't need to specify the type of code. But the *license* can limit the recipient to object code: "Provider hereby grants recipient a license to reproduce and use the Software, in object code format." For an example, see Section 3(a) of the Appendix, on page 127. (And see the footnote on page 12 for definitions of "object code" and "source code.")

2   The copyright law is found at Title 17 of the United States Code ("U.S.C."), starting with Section 101.

Just to muddy the waters, some software is patented, as well as copyrighted. But you only need a patent license if the recipient wants to use software's underlying innovations to create its own software, or to create some other technology. If not, a copyright license should provide all the necessary rights. Patent licenses lie outside the scope of this book. (But this book does touch on patent licenses under *Software Ownership, Assignments*, Subsection I.D.1, on page 33, and *Work-for-Hire*, Subsection I.D.2 on page 35.)

Provider grants Recipient a license: (a) to use the Software and to publicly display and perform it on the worldwide web; (b) to reproduce the Software to the extent reasonably necessary for such purposes; and (c) to sublicense the rights granted in Subsections (a) and (b) to SubCo, Inc. Recipient will not modify the Software, distribute the Software to any third party other than SubCo, Inc., or exercise any copyright holder's rights not specifically granted in this Section. This Agreement grants Recipient no title to or ownership of the Software.

Provider grants Recipient a license to distribute to the public the copies of the Software and to use, publicly perform, and publicly display the Software at any trade show or other marketing venue. Recipient will not, without limitation, modify the Software, sublicense any of the rights granted in this Section, or reproduce the Software except as strictly necessary for the exercise of the rights granted in the preceding sentence. Provider retains full title to and ownership of the Software.

Here are the copyright license rights:

- *Reproduce:* The right to make copies. The license may authorize one copy, a thousand, or any number, including "such copies as are necessary for Recipient's business operations." See all three examples in the clause box above.

- *Modify* or *Create Derivative Works:* The right to change a copyrighted work, creating a new version. See all three examples in the clause box. (The recipient—or whoever wrote the modifications—owns the new code in the derivative work. But the provider owns part of the derivative work too: the original software.)

- *Distribute:* The right to hand out copies, for payment or for free. This right is necessary for software distributors, including resellers. See all three examples in the clause box.[3]

---

3   The copyright statute actually talks about distribution "to the public" (17 U.S.C. Section 106(3)). Legal scholars disagree about whether that means more limited distribution is authorized. Assuming you have the right to make two copies, *Footnote continued on next page.*

Licenses that *forbid* distribution sometimes impose a related restriction: "Recipient will not sell or otherwise transfer possession of any copy of the software, pursuant to 17 U.S.C. Section 109." The point is to forbid transfers under copyright law's "first sale doctrine," which in some cases grants a recipient the right to sell or give away its own single copy of a software application, even without a distribution license. (The law on the first sale doctrine isn't settled, so it's not clear whether the restriction will work. But for providers, it's usually worth a try.)

- *Publicly Perform:* The right to perform a copyrighted work—to present a movie or play, or to read a novel aloud in a commercial setting. This right has not traditionally applied to software. But software used to run a website is arguably performed for the public.[4] The same goes for software demonstrated at a trade show. See all three examples in the clause box above.

- *Publicly Display:* The right to show copies to the public. This right has traditionally applied more to visual images than to software. But software running a website[5]—or demonstrated at a trade show—can often be considered displayed, just as it can be considered performed. See all three examples in the clause box above.

- *Sublicense:* The right to pass license rights on to third parties. The license clause could authorize the recipient to take one or more of the rights granted and pass them on to its own customers or distributors or whomever. See all three examples in the clause box above. (The right to sublicense is sometimes confused with the right to distribute. Distribution rights allow the recipient to hand out *copies*, not to transfer *rights*. However, sublicensing rights are sometimes implied by distribu-

---

for instance, can you give them to friends without a license granting distribution rights? Providers can avoid any doubt by broadly forbidding distribution, as in the second example in the clause box.

4   For website software, public performance rights might be implied even if not specified. If the recipient gets the right to use software, and the key use involves running a website, the recipient can probably do that. The right to reproduce might carry the same implication—because why would the recipient reproduce the software if not to run a website? But for the recipient, it's always better to clarify the rights received.

5   See the preceding footnote for implied rights to display—which operate the same way as implied rights to perform.

tion rights, when the distributor has to give its customers the right to reproduce the software. So the two terms can overlap.)

• *Use (a pseudo right):* The right to run software. See the first and last examples in the clause box above. The exact meaning of "use," however, isn't clear. That's because, unlike the license rights listed above, "use" isn't found in or implied by the copyright statute. Is "use" just the right to run software, or does it overlap the other license rights? For instance, if the license grants only the right to use, can the recipient also repro- duce the software, or publicly perform it? Unless the contract spells it out, the answer will depend on the context—on whether those other rights are necessary to *use* the software.

Just to increase the confusion, legal scholars debate whether "use" even belongs in a copyright license. "Use" is not one of the exclusive rights the law grants copyright holders, so recipients might not need it. After all, you don't need a license to *use* a copyrighted book—to read it.

Despite those issues, you shouldn't hesitate to include the *use pseudo- right* in your contracts. In fact, many recipients will insist on it. And though the law is not yet clear, granting the pseudo-right may have some legal value for the provider.[6] But handle "use" with care. If you're the provider, make sure to list the copyright license rights that are *not* granted. That way, you confirm that "use" does not include any rights you didn't intend. For instance: "Provider grants Recipient a license to reproduce and use ten copies of the Software, but Recipient may not dis- tribute, modify, publicly perform, or publicly display the Software." And if you're the recipient, make sure the license specifically grants the *other* rights you need—the rights to reproduce, distribute, etc.—as well as the right to use. Don't assume the pseudo-right will cover all your needs.

---

6   By granting the right to "use," the clause helps establish that the recipient doesn't *own* its copy of the software. An owner wouldn't need a license to use its copy, just as the owner of a copy of a book doesn't need a license to read it (use it), even if the book's copyrighted. So the recipient of a use license must *not* be an owner, the IT industry argues. That has advantages for the provider. For instance, if the recipient owned its copy, it might not have to return or delete the software when the contract terminates, or even stop using it. (See *Term and Termination, Effects of Termination,* Section II.R.4, on page 113.) And if it owned a copy, the recipient might be able to give that copy to someone else, under copyright law's "first sale doctrine" (17 U.S.C. Section 109). But if the recipient has nothing more than a license, it has none of those own- ership rights.

2. Scope Terms

Scope terms add extra detail to a copyright license, once the copyright holder's rights have been granted or denied.

Copyright Licenses with Scope Terms

Provider grants Recipient a license to reproduce 5 copies of the Software and to use such copies for "service bureau" processing of third party data; provided: (a) Recipient will install such copies only on the computers listed on Attachment A, and (b) Recipient will not use any copy of the Software to process more than 5,000 Transactions per day.

—

Provider grants Distributor an exclusive license to distribute the Licensed Product in the states of Texas and Arkansas.

—

Provider hereby grants Recipient a perpetual, irrevocable, worldwide, non-transferable, nonexclusive, fully-paid, royalty-free license to reproduce, use, and modify the Licensed Software.

Scope terms are limited only by your imagination. Once you've granted rights to the software, you can restrict or define them in almost any way, or not at all.

These are the most typical scope terms:

- *Restrictions on Use:* The provider can limit the recipient to certain uses of the copyrighted work. Software providers often restrict recipients to "internal use." But the license clause can do just the opposite, authorizing "service bureau use"—meaning the recipient can process its customers' data—as in the first example in the clause box above. Providers also limit recipients to certain computers, or to set numbers of transactions or human users. The first example in the clause box limits both computers and transactions. The following limits users: "Recipient may reproduce the Software, provided no more than thirty (30) users access or operate it during any Business Day." If your deal requires restrictions on use, don't hesitate to get creative about drafting them. For instance, the following would be perfectly legitimate: "Recipient agrees not to use the Software on the first Monday of any calendar month, not to install the Software on any computer used to process pet food inventories, and not to permit access to the Software by anyone other than a podiatrist certified to practice in the State of Maryland."

Restrictions on use are distinct from *grants* of the pseudo-right to use, described in the last bullet point of Subsection 1, on page 24. Once the license grants the necessary copyright holders' rights—rights to reproduce, modify, use, etc.—it can turn around and *restrict* the recipient's use of the software. Essentially, the provider says: "OK, I'll grant you the right to reproduce the software"—or to use the software or whatever—"but only if you promise *not* to use it for certain purposes."

- *Exclusivity:* License rights may be exclusive to the recipient. The provider is promising not to grant the same rights to anyone else. So in the second example in the clause box above, the right to distribute in Texas and Arkansas is exclusive to the recipient (Distributor). Or the license clause might do the opposite. The recipient might receive a "nonexclusive" right to distribute, reproduce, etc., as in the last example in the clause box. (It's not always necessary to specify that a license is nonexclusive, but it never hurts to be clear.)[7]

- *Territory:* This scope term restricts license rights to certain areas: usually geographic, but sometimes defined by industry. The second example in the clause box above uses a geographic territory (Texas and Arkansas). The following uses a territory defined by industry: "Distributor may distribute the Licensed Product within the Dental Office Equipment Market." On the other hand, if you want to clarify that there are *no* territorial restrictions, the license should be "worldwide," as in the last example in the clause box. (The term "worldwide" is not strictly necessary because the law will usually assume a license has no territorial limits, but it never hurts to be clear.)

- *Duration:* Unless the contract provides otherwise, license rights last as long as the term of the agreement. But a license can last longer than the

---

7   Exclusivity has some consequences. For one, the recipient *owns* the transferred right; it owns a piece of the copyright. So the recipient can sue third parties for infringement of that particular right. In other words, if the recipient has an exclusive right to distribute in Virginia, and someone else distributes in Virginia, the recipient has legal standing to sue that person. (To help enforce their rights, and for other reasons, recipients with exclusive licenses should consider registering their licenses with the U.S. Copyright Office.)

underlying contract, or it can end earlier. The end of a license can be pegged to a calendar date or to a date to be determined. Here is a date to be determined: "The license rights granted in this Section 2 will continue so long as Recipient is a party to a services contract with Provider's subsidiary, Neeto-Service, Inc." Another option is a "perpetual" license, as in the last example in the clause box above. With a perpetual license, the underlying contract may terminate—ending the recipient's payment obligations and most other promises—but the license rights last forever, unless they're revoked. (The termination clause should confirm that "perpetual" really means "survives termination," to remove any doubt. See *Term and Termination, Effects of Termination,* Subsection II.R.4, on page 113.)

- *Revocability:* If a license is "irrevocable," the provider can't take it away, even if the recipient breaches the contract. If the recipient doesn't pay, the provider's only remedy is to sue for the money. The provider has given up any right to a court order forcing the recipient to stop using the software. At least, that's the generally understood meaning of "irrevocable." But courts' interpretations will vary. Recipients can increase their chances of a broad interpretation by clarifying: "Provider's remedies for breach, including breach of Recipient's payment obligations, may include monetary damages, but Provider hereby waives any right to termination of the license granted in this Section 2."[8] Providers, on the other hand, can protect themselves with terms that delay irrevocability until payment: "The license granted in this Section will become irrevocable upon Recipient's payment of the License Fee." (An irrevocable license is not necessarily perpetual. The provider can't revoke the rights, but the contract might still specify a natural expiration date.)

- *Payment Scope:* A "royalty-free" license, like the last example in the clause box above, requires no royalty payments. That doesn't necessarily mean the recipient gets the license for free. The contract might call for a fixed payment or for payment under some other scheme (usually

---

8   "Irrevocable" licenses actually can be revoked in one of two ways. First, the copyright statute lets the author (the programmer) revoke a license after thirty-five years, no matter what any contract says. Usually, no one cares after that long. Second, it's always possible that a court won't honor irrevocability, particularly if the recipient refuses to pay and has no good reason. Courts don't like clauses that seem unfair.

appearing in the payment clause, not the license clause). The point is that the recipient doesn't have to pay more every time it makes a copy or otherwise exercises its license rights. If the license is "fully paid," also like the last example in the clause box, the parties agree that whatever payments are required, if any, have already been made as of the moment the license is granted. If the license is effective "upon Recipient's payment of the License Fee," for instance, and there are no royalties, the license is "fully paid" when granted. (When used together, as in the last example, the two terms provide overlapping protection for recipients.)

- *Transferability:* A license clause can provide that the rights granted are "non-transferable," as in the last example in the clause box above. In other words, the recipient can't give the license to anyone else. Or the clause can say that the license *is* "transferable," meaning the recipient *can* give it away. Note that sometimes these terms are unnecessary. Most contracts have an assignment clause governing the transfer of rights. If the assignment clause says the contract is or is not transferable ("assignable"), there's no need to repeat it in the license clause.[9] (A transfer is not the same as a sublicense. In a transfer or assignment, the recipient/licensee gives away all its license rights—the whole contract—and is left with none. In a sublicense, the recipient/licensee keeps its rights, but authorizes a third party to use them.)

∗   ∗   ∗   ∗

Scope terms may apply to all the license rights granted or only to some. For instance, the right to reproduce software may be perpetual, while the right to distribute it lasts only one year. Or the right to distribute software may be exclusive within a particular territory, while the right to distribute outside that territory is nonexclusive.

---

9   See *Assignment*, Section III.I, on page 121. Note that there are two kinds of "assignments." Here, we're talking about an assignment of an entire contract, with all its rights and obligations. "Assignment" also refers to a transfer of ownership rights in a copyright or other intellectual property. (For that sort of assignment, see *Software Ownership: Assignment and Work-for-Hire*, Assignments, Subsection I.D.1, on page 33.)

    If the license rights are non-transferable, but the entire contract is assignable, what you have is a mess. The two clauses contradict each other, at least arguably, and it's hard to say which governs.

Scope terms should appear in the license clause itself. That makes the contract easier to understand. But you may run into contracts with scope terms spread around, so read every word.

3. Unrestricted License

An unrestricted license throws in the kitchen sink. The provider grants all the rights of copyright holders, with a broad scope. The license authorizes the recipient to do just about anything with the software, but the provider still owns it and can grant licenses to third parties.

Recipients sometimes want these super-broad licenses when they pay for software development. Usually, an unrestricted license costs less than full ownership—than an outright purchase of the copyright.

Unrestricted Copyright License

Provider hereby grants Recipient a perpetual, irrevocable, worldwide, transferable, fully-paid, royalty-free, non-exclusive license: (a) to reproduce, modify, distribute, publicly perform, publicly display, and use the Licensed Software; and (b) to sublicense any or all such rights to third parties.

It is actually possible to draft a license that's even broader than the example in the clause box above. One or more of the rights granted could be exclusive. If *all* the rights were exclusive, however, the seller would have no copyright left. The transaction would work like an assignment, a transfer of copyright ownership to the recipient, despite the word "license."[10]

4. Open Source License

"Open source" licenses include rights to use and modify source code, at no extra charge.[11] Beyond that, there is no clear, widely-accepted definition of "open source." Most IT professionals associate the term with public access to source code. So a license that grants source code access to the recipient, but doesn't make it available to third parties, generally won't be considered open source.

Open source doesn't necessarily mean "free software." The recipient might have to pay for its rights to a copy. But the recipient is "free" to access and change the source code, and sometimes free to make additional copies of the software.

---

10 See *Software Ownership: Assignment and Work-for-Hire*, Section I.D, on page 32.

11 See the footnote on page 12 for a definition of "source code."

Some open source providers post their source code on the web and grant broad rights to anyone who downloads it. In these cases, the license might include rights and scope terms like those of the unrestricted license in the clause box in Subsection 3, page 29—with source code added to the definition of "Licensed Software." That structure essentially puts the source code in the public domain. Recipients can use the source code to modify the software or to incorporate it into other products.

Some open source licenses, however, include a key restriction in the scope terms. If the recipient modifies the software, it can't charge third parties for the modified version.

Distribution Rights with "Copyleft" Scope Terms

Recipient may use, reproduce, and create derivative works of the Software. Recipient may distribute a derivative work of the Software, provided: (a) such derivative work is distributed free of charge, except that Recipient may charge a fee for transferring a single copy; (b) such derivative work is licensed to third parties pursuant to the terms of this Agreement, including this Agreement's grant of modification and distribution rights; and (c) Recipient provides full and complete source code with any copy of such derivative work.

The example in the clause box is part of a "copyleft" license—so named because it turns copy*right* protection around. To use the open source software, the recipient has to give up most of its copyright protections for new products that incorporate the software (derivative works). It can't charge a fee for distribution of the new product, and its customers can further distribute and modify the new product—as can the *customers'* customers.

Copyleft scope terms are usually fine for recipients who don't care about selling rights in software—who just want to use it. But they can be deadly for software distributors. In fact, copyleft licenses are often called "viral" because they infect any program combined with the original software. If the recipient includes even a small amount of copyleft software in a new product, it arguably can't charge for the new product. This viral effect is particularly deadly when the recipient puts time and energy into creating a software application, and some employee includes a small piece of copyleft software without telling anyone. The whole application may lose most of its copyright protection—and can't be licensed for a fee.

Of course, copyleft scope terms don't completely remove the recipient's right to make money on new products. It can still charge customers a fee for the original copy (per subsection (a) in the clause box), even though customers can then modify and distribute at will. And it can charge for software maintenance and other support services. Plus, the recipient may get something in return for giving up copyright protection. Open source advocates say copyleft software is better, because more people can see the source code and improve it.[12]

---

12 For more on open source licenses, look up the Open Source Initiative (www.open-source.org). The Initiative is a nonprofit organization that advocates copyleft licensing. It certifies licensing contracts, giving its stamp of approval to well-known agreements like the "GNU GPA" and the Mozilla Public License. (The example in the clause box above has not been reviewed or certified by the Open Source Initiative.)

D. Software Ownership: Assignment and Work-for-Hire

Software contracts address ownership through assignments of intellectual property and work-for-hire clauses. Assignments transfer ownership from provider to recipient. Work-for-hire, on the other hand, doesn't transfer ownership because the provider isn't the owner and never was. Under a work-for-hire clause, the recipient owns the software from the moment it's written.

This section differs from all others in this book. It offers only partial coverage of its topic because ownership transfers are too big and complicated for this short format. A lot can go wrong with ownership clauses, particularly for the recipient and particularly when patents are involved. Recipients' attorneys craft long clauses to protect their clients, but they still face the risk that their transfers will fail, at least in part. This section doesn't discuss recipients' risks in detail or provide the more extensive clauses. You should address those issues with an experienced lawyer. However, this section does give you an overview of ownership transfers and the issues they raise. No education on software and services contracts would be complete without that. Also, some ownership transfers *are* simple enough for this format, so the example clauses below will serve recipients in those situations. And the clauses below will *usually* serve providers, since they face less risk in transfer situations. Finally, if you do get help from an experienced IT contracts lawyer, this section should help you ask good questions.

    *   *   *   *

For recipients, work-for-hire clauses are better than assignments because they can't be revoked. Effective patent assignments are difficult to revoke too, but copyright assignments can be revoked after thirty-five years—no matter what the contract says. On the other hand, work-for-hire clauses only operate when the provider serves as the recipient's employee, and under a few other limited circumstances. See Subsection 2 below.

Before executing an assignment or work-for-hire contract, the recipient should ask itself why it wants to *own* the software. Often recipients paying for software development argue: "We paid to make it, so we own it." But if the recipient only plans to *use* the application—if it doesn't sell software—it may get little value from ownership. A license might provide all the rights the recipient needs, particularly if it's an "unrestricted license," like the one in Subsection I.C.3. And the provider might charge less for a license, because if it retains ownership, it can generate additional revenue granting licenses to third parties.[1]

As with licenses, the contract should clearly define the "Software"—or whatever you're calling the application in question. If there is any chance of dispute about the content of the software, make sure to list all modules, libraries, big-fixes, etc. Generally, the definition should specify all forms of code: object code, source code, etc. It might also include any documentation necessary to understand the software. For instance: "'Software' refers to the DuckTracker software application to be created pursuant to this Agreement, including without limitation: (i) all versions thereof; (ii) object code, source code, machine code, and all other forms of software code; and (iii) all user manuals and related technical documentation."[2]

1. Assignments

An assignment clause states that the provider "hereby assigns" its rights to the recipient.[3] The rest of the clause addresses the many things that can go wrong.

---

1   See *Software Licenses in General, Unrestricted License*, Subsection I.C.3, on page 29. Licenses do have a key disadvantage. A license is a contract right, and contracts can be terminated. An assignment or work-for-hire clause, on the other hand, grants an ownership right, and ownership generally can't be terminated (except after thirty-five years, in the case of copyright assignments, as explained above). But with a good license, the risk of termination should be minimal—particularly if the license provides that it's irrevocable and perpetual.

2   For definitions of "object code" and "source code," see the footnote on page 12. For documentation, see *Documentation*, Section II.L, on page 96.

    Recipients of both assignments and work-for-hire clauses should consider registering their copyrights with the U.S. Copyright Office.

3   Note that there are two kinds of "assignments." Here, we're talking about a transfer of ownership rights in a copyright or other intellectual property. "Assignment" also refers to the transfer of an entire contract, with all its rights and obligations. (For that sort of assignment, see *Assignment*, Section III.I, on page 121.)

Assignment

(a) Provider hereby assigns to Recipient all of its right, title, and interest in and to the Software, including without limitation all rights arising out of U.S. patent law and U.S. copyright law, or any foreign equivalent of either, and including any registration, application, extension, reversion, or resurrection. Provider will execute such documents as Recipient reasonably requests and otherwise cooperate with Recipient to confirm such assignment, at Recipient's expense.

(b) To the extent that any element of the Software cannot be assigned to Recipient pursuant to Subsection (a) above, Provider hereby grants Recipient a perpetual, irrevocable, fully-paid, royalty-free, worldwide license to reproduce, create derivative works from, distribute, publicly display, publicly perform, make, have made, offer for sale, sell or otherwise dispose of, import, and use the Software, with the right to sublicense each and every such right.

(c) Provider will require that all its employees and contractors in any way involved in creating the Software execute assignment agreements with Recipient in the form attached hereto as Exhibit A. Provider will reasonably cooperate with Recipient in assuring such employees' and contractors' compliance with the terms of Exhibit A.

(d) The rights and obligations of this Section will survive any termination or expiration of this Agreement.

The example in the clause box assigns all forms of intellectual property, including both patents and copyright. But if you're the recipient and you really care about patent ownership, you should seek additional legal help. Patent assignments are full of pitfalls, so their clauses often include additional terms protecting the recipient. But if your main interest is copyrights, the clause above is a good example. It's meant to grant full copyright ownership and the right to exploit the software in just about any way you can imagine.[4]

---

4   If the copyright assignment is effective but the patent assignment is not, the recipient becomes the exclusive owner of that particular software application. It can keep others from reproducing the code. But the recipient can't patent the *innovations* built into the code. And the recipient probably won't be able to keep others from writing new software applications that use those innovations. (Most contracts should include a severability clause, addressing potentially unenforceable terms, like the patent assignment at issue here. See *Severability*, Section III.K, on page 122.)

Sometimes, courts and government agencies won't honor an assignment unless the provider signs special forms or cooperates in other ways. It's hard to know in advance what kind of cooperation you will need. So subsection (a) in the clause box above requires whatever reasonable cooperation the recipient may eventually request.

Even with the provider's cooperation, assignments sometimes don't work. Some jurisdictions, particularly certain foreign ones, bend over backwards to protect authors from their own contracts and won't fully enforce assignments. So a good assignment clause includes a royalty-free backup license, as in subsection (b) above. The license grants the recipient full rights to exploit the software, even if it doesn't get full ownership. (Subsection (b) grants both copyright license rights and patent license rights.)

Subsections (a) and (b) assume the provider wrote the software. But what if the provider has employees or contractors who worked on the project, or *will* work on it? Did each contributor execute a valid assignment or work-for-hire contract, giving the provider full rights it can then transfer to the recipient? If not, those contributors will own part of the software. If the recipient has any doubt about employee or contractor rights, it should have them sign separate assignments. That's why subsection (c) above requires separate contracts from each contributor. The form for these separate assignment contracts would be an attachment to the main agreement, and its central clause would be identical to subsections (a) and (b). (But replace "Provider" with something like "Assignor.")[5]

2. Work-for-Hire

In general, the author of software (or of any writing) owns it. If a recipient wants intellectual property ownership, it needs an assignment. But with a work-for-hire clause, the recipient owns the copyright from the moment it's written.

---

5   Note that Subsection (c) in the clause box gives the recipient a contract right against the provider, not against the employees (or independent contractors). If the employees never actually sign their separate assignment contracts, the recipient can sue the provider for breach of contract, but it may not be able to get any ownership rights from the employees.

     Some state laws restrict employers' rights to require assignments of inventions. If in doubt about your state, get experienced legal help.

Work-for-hire applies to copyrights only: it can't allocate patent rights. However, many work-for-hire clauses, like the example in the clause box below, include backup assignments that do transfer patent rights.

A work-for-hire clause will only work if it passes one of two tests. First, the provider has to be the recipient's employee and has to write the software within the scope of his or her employment. Or second, if the provider is not an employee, the software has to fit into one of copyright law's nine "eligible" categories, listed below. Many software deals don't pass either test. For them, a work-for-hire clause would be null and void.

The first test is simple, so long as there can be no doubt about the provider's employment status. If the provider is an employee—and his or her job requires the type of software programming in question—the deal passes the first test. In fact, a written contract isn't entirely necessary, since the law will generally consider the employment a work-for-hire relationship. But it's better to avoid any doubt by including a work-for-hire clause in the employment contract, or if that agreement isn't in writing, by signing a stand-alone work-for-hire contract.

It's often hard to tell whether a relationship qualifies as "employment." What if the provider serves part-time, or works from home with no health benefits? Unfortunately, neither the courts nor Congress has given us a clear test for employment. Courts consider thirteen factors in deciding employment status—and you can never be sure how much a court will care about each factor. So if you want to use work-for-hire and you're not absolutely sure the provider is an employee, consider some experienced legal help.

The second test allows work-for-hire treatment, even if the provider isn't an employee, if the software is ordered "as a contribution to a collective work, as a part of a motion picture or other audiovisual work, as a translation, as a supplementary work [like a book's introduction], as a compilation, as an instructional text, as a test, as answer material for a test, or as an atlas."[6] Software can deliver tests, instructional texts, and atlases, so those categories will work for some deals. Audiovisual software may also pass the second test. And the "contribution to a collective work" category could do the trick where multiple programmers create a single software application. But if in doubt about any of the category definitions, seek additional help.

---

6   17 U.S.C. Section 101. The law also provides that, to pass the second test, the parties must "expressly agree in a written instrument signed by them that the work shall be considered a work made for hire."

Work-For-Hire

(a) The Software will be considered a work made for hire pursuant to the U.S. Copyright Act, 17 U.S.C. §101 *et seq*, and will be Company's sole property.

(b) To the extent that the software incorporates any inventions or innovations that may not be considered works of authorship, and to the extent any element of the Software may not be considered a work made for hire under applicable law, Programmer hereby assigns to Company all of its right, title, and interest in and to the Software, including without limitation all rights arising out of U.S. patent law and U.S. copyright law, or any foreign equivalent of either, and including any registration, application, extension, reversion, or resurrection. Programmer will execute such documents as Company reasonably requests and otherwise cooperate with Company to confirm such assignment, at Company's expense.

(c) To the extent that Subsections (a) and (b) above do not provide Company with full right, title, and interest in and to the Software, if any, Programmer hereby grants Company a perpetual, irrevocable, fully-paid, royalty-free, worldwide license to reproduce, create derivative works from, distribute, publicly display, publicly perform, make, have made, offer for sale, sell or otherwise dispose of, import, and use the Software, with the right to sublicense each and every such right.

(d) The rights and obligations of this Section will survive any termination or expiration of this Agreement.

The example in the clause box above uses "Company" and "Programmer" for recipient and provider, respectively. If it appears in an employment contract, you might want to replace "Company" and "Programmer" with "Employer" and "Employee."

Most of the example's terms address the consequences of failure. What happens if some court will not accept the software's work-for-hire status? The example has two backups: an assignment, subsection (b), and an unrestricted license, subsection (c). Any element of the software that isn't subject to work-for-hire treatment is *assigned* to the recipient. And if anything isn't subject to the work-for-hire clause *and* isn't assignable, the license should still cover it. The recipient might not own the software, but it can still reproduce it, distribute it, etc.

In the example above, the backup assignment and license give the recipient patent rights, as well as copyright holders' rights. But as subsection 1 above explains, on page 33, patent assignments are complicated, and many related issues lie outside the scope of this book, so the example might not be sufficient.

E. Promise of Professional Services

In a services contract, the provider agrees to help the recipient. This section addresses *professional* services.[1]

This book distinguishes professional services from machine-based services. The two overlap, but in general, professional services rely on people. A human being is the service-provider, though he or she may use a computer. Professional services include computer programming, computer maintenance, tech support, and consulting. Machine-based services, on the other hand, rely almost entirely on computers. For instance, you might call your Internet service provider and talk to a human (if you can get through), but the human doesn't provide the real service. A computer connects you to the Internet, so Internet connectivity is a machine-based service. So are online security, web hosting, collocation, and application service provider systems. Section I.F, on page 47, addresses machine-based services.

A professional service clause says, essentially: "Provider will provide the following services to Recipient: _____." This section addresses the blank: the terms defining the service. This section also addresses midstream changes in the service, terms for multiple services (multiple statements of work), and terms covering service-provider experience.

Some contracts feature both a professional services clause and a license (or a transfer of software ownership). In many end-user software contracts, for instance, the license clause grants the recipient rights to software while a maintenance clause promises professional services. Technology development contracts also include both services and IP grants. The *service* is the creation of

---

1   In a professional services contract, the provider is an independent contractor, not the recipient's employee. But the line between contractor and employee isn't always clear, and misclassifications can cause legal trouble. So consider consulting an employment lawyer if you have doubts.

software or other technology. And a license grants the recipient rights to exploit that technology. This section doesn't address licenses or other IP transfers. For those clauses, see: *Standard End-User Software License*, Section I.A, on page 12; *Software Licenses in General*, Section I.C, on page 20; and *Software Ownership: Assignment and Work-for-Hire*, Section I.D, on page 32.

1. Defining the Service

Services descriptions vary widely.

Description of Services

During Business Hours, Provider will staff the Help Desk with no fewer than two (2) technicians. Such technicians will exercise their best efforts to resolve computer and user errors promptly, in response to Recipient technical support requests.

—

Throughout the term of this Agreement, Provider will: (a) make 3 Consultants available to Recipient during Business Hours to advise on system integration; and (b) produce a system development report 30 or more days after the end of each calendar quarter, providing detailed descriptions of system development progress.

—

Provider will write an employee benefits software application that conforms to the technical specifications set forth in Exhibit A (the "Software"). Provider is not required to provide support or maintenance for the Software except to the extent provided in Subsection 6(a) (Warranty).

—

Provider will maintain the System so that it performs according to its technical specifications, listed on the System Website, during no less than ninety-eight percent (98%) of each calendar month.

Services descriptions can be task-driven or outcome-driven. Task-driven descriptions favor the provider. In clauses like the first two examples in the box above, all the provider has to do is perform the tasks listed. "Provider will provide two employees to do the following...." The recipient might be unhappy with the outcome, but that's not the provider's problem.

Outcome-driven descriptions, like the last two examples in the clause box, favor the recipient. "Provider will achieve the following outcomes...." The provider can't point to a list of tasks and say: "I tried." If the provider doesn't achieve the outcome, it hasn't met its obligations.

Many contracts put the services description in an attachment. For long descriptions, that's usually a good idea because it simplifies the contract. The attachment may be called the "Statement of Work," or just "Exhibit B." The contract can simply state: "Provider will provide the services listed on Exhibit B."

Clarity is particularly important in services descriptions, and particularly difficult. On fixed price deals, providers often suffer from "scope creep": the job gets bigger but the price doesn't. A clear description of the services helps prevent scope creep, because the provider can say: "Look, that's not included in the contract; it'll cost extra." Recipients should protect themselves from unclear descriptions too. They should make sure the contract promises all the expected help. So in defining the service, make sure the parties really imagine the same tasks. Is tech support required? Or is it excluded, as in the third example in the clause box? How about quality assurance? Bug fixes? After-hours support? Is special equipment required, and if so, who supplies it? Think through all possible sources of dispute or misunderstanding, and define any debatable terms.[2]

2. Change Orders and Midstream Terminations

Often, the recipient wants to change the services part-way through the project, or terminate them. This subsection addresses both change orders and midstream termination.

---

2 One common error is to include the recipient's tasks in the services description. For instance: "Provider will provide the following services: (1) Recipient's project manager will meet with Provider by June 17 and outline the specifications...." That makes no sense because the provider can't make the recipient show up at that meeting. To avoid confusion, the recipient's tasks should be listed separately—in their own attachment or clause.

> ### Change Order Clauses
>
> The parties may agree to additional or modified services through a written change order, and such change order will become part of this Agreement when executed by both parties.
>
> —
>
> Recipient may request that Provider add features to the Software not in the Technical Specifications by submitting a written change order to Provider, in the form attached hereto as Exhibit B. Provider will negotiate in good faith regarding price and other terms related to such additional features, and any change order will become part of this Agreement when executed by both parties.

A change order system lets the parties add additional services without a new contract. See both examples in the clause box above. You don't really need a change order; you could just amend the contract to add new services. But a change order procedure is easier. For the provider, it offers an easy way to add new revenues to a project. And for the recipient, clauses like the second example above require that the provider negotiate in good faith. The "good faith" commitment doesn't mean a lot, but the provider at least promises to consider the recipient's request, and to quote a reasonable price.

If you do create a change-order procedure, consider a change order *form*, as in the second example in the clause box. That way, a casual exchange of letters or e-mails won't count as a change order. The form could read: "Pursuant to the March 13, 2006 Technology Services Agreement between Obsequio, Inc. ("Provider") and ScopeCreep LLC ("Recipient"), Provider will provide the additional services listed below, and Recipient will pay the additional fees listed below...." Or, you could create a more elaborate form. If you'd like a more elaborate model, see the statement of work form in the second clause box in Subsection 3 below, on page 45. If you use that model, replace "Statement of Work" with "Change Order" throughout the form.[3]

---

3   Change orders usually apply to changes in project scope, while statements of work apply to whole new projects. But beyond that difference, the two are similar. So if change orders play a major role in your contract, review Subsection 3 on multiple statements of work, starting with page 43 below.

What if, instead of changing the project, the recipient kills it? Many contracts have a termination for convenience clause, allowing one party to end a project without breaching the contract. As Section II.R on *Term and Termination* explains, the party terminating for convenience often has to compensate the other for lost time, resources, etc.[4] But in a professional services contract requiring cooperation, the recipient could end the project without formally terminating for convenience. In other words, the recipient could terminate and escape any compensation obligations. For instance, the provider might need to meet with the recipient's chief technology officer to provide the services. What if the recipient makes the CTO unavailable, or fires him or her—with no formal termination? If the provider did a good job drafting the services description, that will count as breach of contract. But it's hard to anticipate every risk in a services description. So providers should consider a backup clause addressing midstream termination.

Midstream Termination

Recipient's failure to provide the staff required by the Statement of Work for any Recipient task or joint task, within ten (10) business days of Provider's written request, will constitute termination of this Agreement for convenience pursuant to Subsection 13(c) below.

——

Recipient's failure to make the Facility available to Provider's personnel for more than five (5) business days out of any calendar month will constitute a material breach of this Agreement.

Midstream termination clauses protect providers by closing the "non-cooperation" loophole. The recipient's failure to cooperate counts as termination for convenience, as in the first example in the clause box, or breach of contract, as in the second.

3. Multiple Statements of Work

Often, the parties plan on several projects over a long period, and they can't identify all the work when they draft the contract. Some recipients and providers handle this by negotiating an amendment to the contract for each

---

4   See *Term and Termination, Termination for Convenience*, Subsection II.R.3, on page 112.

new project. That's messy and confusing. A better solution is the multiple statements of work format. The contract acts as an umbrella—a master services agreement—and it doesn't have to be amended. When the parties agree on a new project, they fill out a new statement of work.

Multiple Statement of Work Procedure

Provider will provide such services as are required by any statement of work in the form attached hereto as Attachment A, executed by each party ("Statement of Work"). Upon execution, a Statement of Work will become part of this Agreement. In the even of any conflict with a Statement of Work, the terms of this main body of this Agreement will govern.

The body of the contract should set up the statement of work procedure, as in the example in the clause box above. It's usually best to include a statement of work *form* to fill out, again as in the example. (See below for statement of work forms.) That's better than letting the parties use any old Word document, e-mail, notepad, or napkin. Use of a form helps keep careless employees from agreeing to new projects without realizing it, and without proper review. Some clauses go further and provide: "No statement of work will become part of this Agreement or bind either party unless signed by each party's Project Manager" (or some other senior officer).

What if a statement of work contradicts the main body of the contract? What if the statement says the provider owns all IP rights in the work product, but the contract says the recipient does? Conflicts like that should be rare, because statements of work should stick to project details and avoid issues already addressed in the contract. But mistakes happen. The best remedy is a clause providing that, in case of conflict, the contract overrules the statement of work, as in the example in the clause box. That protects your hard-won contract from careless revision through the statement of work process. If the parties really want to change the contract, they can amend it. Usually, an amendment involves more review, so you can make sure no one is giving away the farm.

Some companies, however, want maximum flexibility in their statement of work process, and they let the statement of work trump the contract. I think that's a bad idea. But if you insist, make sure to limit the reach of the statements of work, in the contract's main body: "The terms of a Statement of Work will govern in the event of a conflict with the terms of this Agreement, but only with respect to the work set forth in such Statement of Work and not with respect to any other work to be performed pursuant to this Agreement, including without limitation pursuant to any other Statement of Work."[5]

Statement of Work Form[6]

STATEMENT OF WORK NUMBER _____
To Technology Services Agreement
Project Title: _____

This Statement of Work Number ___ (this "Statement of Work") is entered into pursuant to the August 24, 2007 Technology Services Agreement (the "Agreement") by and between Help-U-Cope LLC ("Provider") and TechnoMess Corporation ("Recipient").

I.   *Definitions.* Capitalized terms not otherwise defined in this Statement of Work will have the meanings given in the main body of the Agreement.

II. *Construction.* This Statement of Work is incorporated into the Agreement. In the event of any conflict between this Statement of Work and the main body of the Agreement, the main body will govern. The provisions of this Statement of Work govern only the subject matter hereof and not any other subject-matter covered by the Agreement.

III. *Services & Deliverables.* Provider will provide the following services: _____ *[Insert description of services. Include technical specifications for any technology to be created, or include reference to specifications attached to this Statement of Work.]*

IV. *Recipient Cooperation.* Recipient will reasonably cooperate with Provider in the provision of services and will provide the following assistance to Provider: _____ *[Insert description of Recipient responsibilities, or insert "N/A" if not applicable.]*

V.   *Payment.* Recipient will pay Provider as follows: _____ *[Insert payment schedule. Insert any payment/invoicing terms not already covered in main body of Agreement. If none of the preceding applies, insert: "Client will pay for Services pursuant to the requirements of Section 5 of the Agreement."]*

---

5   For more on conflicts, see *Conflicts among Attachments*, Section III.M, on page 122.

6   This statement of work form is available for download at this book's website: www.TechContracts.net.

> VI. *Additional Provisions.* In addition, the parties agree as follows:
> _____ *[Insert additional*
>   *terms or "N/A" if not applicable.]*
> This Statement of Work is effective as of the latest date of execution set
> forth below.
> ***signature block for both parties***

The statement of work form should give the parties enough flexibility to craft a project. It should also require that each new statement of work get a number, to enable project tracking and management. And the form, once complete, should be signed by both parties. See the example form in the clause box above.

The italicized text in brackets is part of the example form in the clause box. It provides instructions for future statement of work drafters. You never need to remove it; just add the necessary text beneath it.

4. Experience and Qualifications

In many professional services deals, the recipient should make sure the provider assigns qualified people—assuming the recipient isn't an individual providing services without employees. This concern applies most strongly to task-driven services.

> *Qualifications*
>
> All Provider's employees or contractors staffing the Help Desk will have no fewer than two (2) years' full time work experience operating or maintaining DataCrawler databases and will be certified by a Sinecure Corporation authorized trainer for maintenance of PS3 operating systems.

Avoid vague qualifications like "adequate experience." No one knows what that means. Terms like "industry standard experience" work a bit better, if the industry really has a recognized standard. But the best option is to specify concrete qualifications, like the ones in the clause box above.

F. Promise of Machine-Based Services

A machine-based service is a technical service provided through computers and software. These include telecommunications, Internet connectivity, data management, online security, and ASP (application service provider) systems.

Machine-based services and professional services overlap, but in general, the latter rely on people more than on machines. Professional services include technology consulting and software programming. This book addresses them in Section I.E, on page 39.

The promise of machine-based services is a simple clause. The contract names the service—"Internet connectivity," for example, or "IT security"— and the provider promises to provide it.[1]

Description of Services

Provider will provide Recipient with Internet connectivity services, pursuant to Provider's policies listed on the reverse side of the Order Form, as updated from time to time via notice in Provider's monthly newsletter.

—

Provider will provide Recipient with document-sharing services through use of Provider's online software application, CircularFile-Online, according to Provider's then-standard policies and procedures listed at Provider's website.

---

[1] Don't confuse machine-based services with software licenses. In a license, the recipient may, for instance, receive data-tracking software. Data-tracking sounds like a service, but the recipient receives software, not help. The deal becomes a services contract of the *provider* tracks the data, regardless of whose computers or software it uses.

—

Provider will provide information technology security services ("Services") that perform according to the technical specifications listed in Attachment A.

Some contracts promise services but don't describe them. That's a bad idea, except where there can't be much disagreement about the nature of the services. Otherwise, machine-based services should be described in detail. The recipient should be sure what it's getting, and the provider should be sure what it has promised and what it hasn't. The description can appear in the contract's main body, on a website, as in the second example above, or in an attachment, as in the first and last examples. Recipients should hesitate to accept website descriptions or services "provided according to Provider's then-standard policies and procedures." The provider could change the description and reduce service quality. But for "mass" services, sold to large numbers of customers, recipients often have no choice.

Sometimes, detailed services descriptions appear in the contract's technical specifications, as in the last example in the clause box. And some contracts go beyond specifications and list consequences for service failures, in a Service Level Agreement. See *Technical Specifications*, Section II.A, on page 53, and *Service Level Agreements*, Section II.B, on page 57.

G. Payment

Payment terms can take many forms. The examples in the clause box below are just a few.

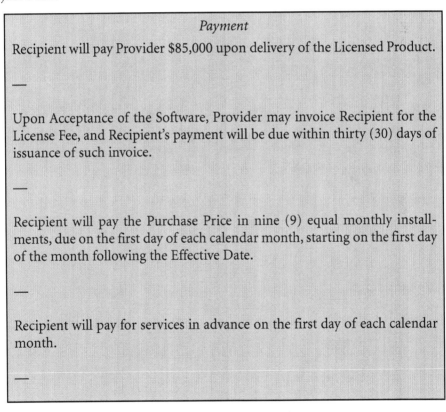

Payment

Recipient will pay Provider $85,000 upon delivery of the Licensed Product.

—

Upon Acceptance of the Software, Provider may invoice Recipient for the License Fee, and Recipient's payment will be due within thirty (30) days of issuance of such invoice.

—

Recipient will pay the Purchase Price in nine (9) equal monthly installments, due on the first day of each calendar month, starting on the first day of the month following the Effective Date.

—

Recipient will pay for services in advance on the first day of each calendar month.

—

> Distributor will pay Provider forty-percent (40%) of all revenues collected from end-user customers for licenses to the Software. On the tenth (10th) Business Day of each calendar quarter, Distributor will report all Software sales for the preceding quarter, including customer names, units sold, and amounts receivable and received. Distributor will include such additional detail as Provider reasonably requests, and will pay all amounts due within thirty (30) days of such report.
>
> ⸻
>
> Recipient will pay for Services on a time and materials basis, according to the rate schedule in Exhibit B. Provider will invoice amounts due on the last day of each calendar quarter. Payment against all invoices will be due within ten (10) days of receipt thereof.

Payment clauses are often simple, but they do hide a few traps for the unwary.

In distribution agreements, royalty obligations can lead to disputes, because the amounts due can't be defined in advance. The solution is detail. Be sure the distributor has to report all sales, in detail and on a regular basis, as in the fifth example in the clause box above. Usually, that's the only way for the provider to learn how much is due.[1] Also, if the provider gets a percentage of revenues, rather than a fixed payment, it should consider setting some minimum royalty: "Regardless of revenues collected, the royalty payment will not fall below $150.00 per unit." Otherwise, the distributor could sell for nothing or next to nothing—as a promotion, for instance—and the provider could get no royalties.

Time and materials clauses generally create a billable hours structure for professional services contracts. The recipient pays for the providers' employees' time and reimburses the provider for equipment and other materials. These clauses work best when the contract specifies the provider's rates, as in the last example in the clause box above. But even a rate schedule doesn't address the issue of excessive costs. What if the provider spends two hundred hours solving a problem the recipient thinks should take twenty? A good solution is a clause providing something like: "Fees will not exceed $12,000 for any given calendar month unless Recipient agrees in writing in advance."

---

1   Software audits give the provider additional security. See *Software Audits*, Section II.J, on page 93.

Another thorny issue arises in software development clauses, where payment is required when the work is done. What does "done" mean? If the provider says it's finished, but the software doesn't do what the recipient wanted, is it done? The best way to address this is through some sort of acceptance procedure, as suggested by the second example above. For acceptance procedures, see *Delivery, Acceptance, and Rejection*, Section II.E, on page 72.

II. General Clauses

"General Clauses" is a catch-all category. The terms below account for most of the ink spread across most software and services contracts. The one characteristic shared by all these clauses is that they generate a lot of disagreement, debate, and compromise.

A. Technical Specifications

Technical specifications describe software and computer systems in detail. They say what the technology will do—how it's supposed to perform. In many contracts, they are the most important terms: the *only* ones that will matter in many disputes. Yet businesspeople and lawyers usually pay them little attention.[1]

Technical specifications ("specs") are appropriate for most software contracts, including licenses, assignments, and distribution agreements. They're also appropriate for any professional services contract that involves the creation or maintenance of software or computer systems. Finally, specs are appropriate for many contracts covering machine-based services (services that rely on computers).[2] In these agreements, the specs describe the service itself: speed of transmission between offices, interface between systems, etc.

A specs clause or attachment is not the same thing as a service level agreement (an "SLA"). SLA's appear in machine-based services contracts. They say what will happen if the service fails—what remedies the recipient has—rather than how the service should operate. You may run into contracts that combine the specs and the SLA into a single clause or attachment. This book, however, addresses them separately. To learn about SLA's, review *Service Level Agreements*, Section II.B, on page 57.

1　Some IT professionals distinguish "functional specifications" and technical specifications. The line between the two is not clear, but in general, functional specs describe software and systems from the user's point of view: how the screen shots should appear, how the computer will respond to a command, etc. Technical specs are more technical, looking at issues like system architecture and programming languages. This book makes no such distinction. It addresses both under this "technical specifications" heading.

2　For the difference between professional and machine-based services, see *Promise of Professional Services*, Section I.E, on page 39, and *Promise of Machine-Based Services*, Section I.G, on page 47.

＊   ＊   ＊   ＊

The specs provide information used in *other* contract clauses. The clause box below contains examples of those other clauses—so that you can see the role of technical specifications.

> ### *Clauses Referring to Technical Specifications*[3]
>
> Provider warrants that, during the first one (1) year after the Effective Date, the Software will perform according to its technical specifications listed in Attachment A.
>
> —
>
> Provider will maintain the System so that it performs materially in accordance with its Specifications.
>
> —
>
> Provider will design a software application that conforms to the technical specifications attached hereto as Exhibit B.
>
> —
>
> After a Level 2 Error, Provider will repair the System, so that it performs in accordance with its Technical Specifications, within 10 hours.
>
> —
>
> In the event that the software fails the acceptance tests, Recipient will provide a written description of each deviation from the specifications listed in Attachment A, and Provider will repair the software so that it performs in accordance with all its specifications.

---

3   For more on the underlying clauses in the box, see, respectively: *Warranty, Warranty of Function*, Subsection II.C.1, on page 61; *Promise of Professional Services, Defining the Service*, Subsection I.E.1, on page 40 (for both the second and third examples); *Service Level Agreements, SLA Remedies*, Subsection II.B.1, on page 57; and *Delivery, Acceptance, and Rejection*, Section II.E, on page 72.

1. The Importance of Specifications

Because specs are so technical, many recipients and providers pay them little attention or leave them out. That's a bad choice.

Imagine you're the recipient and you license a widget-tracking computer system for your factory floor. You quickly discover that the system takes too long to generate reports. Worse, it won't sync with your floor managers' hand-held computers. You complain to the provider, but you signed a contract with no technical specs. All the contract says is that you bought, "WidgetTracker Server Edition 5.02, a computer system for tracking and managing widgets on a factory floor." That doesn't address speed or synchronization. Maybe the provider's salespeople told you the system was fast and could sync, but those promises didn't find their way into the contract, so they don't do you much good.[4]

Now imagine you're the provider. You're a little better off, but not much. You have a customer who thinks you were dishonest, and you have a dispute on your hands. Ideally, you would point to the contract and say: "Look, the contract says what the system does; it's not required to do anything else." But you can't because the contract has no specs. As the provider, you need specs to clarify what the system *will not* do.

In other words, as this book's introduction explains, good fences make good neighbors. Detailed specifications are excellent fences.

There *are* contracts that don't need detailed specifications. If there's little chance reasonable minds could differ about what software is supposed to do, specs are not necessary. For instance, if the deal involves standard off-the-shelf software, with widely-known functions, you can often leave out the details. Or you might just provide: "the System will perform according to its technical specifications published by Provider." That assumes, of course, that the provider has published something.

But if in doubt, assume you need specs.

2. Responsibility for Specifications

Who should draft specifications? Recipient or provider? Lawyer, businessperson, or programmer?

As between recipient and provider, there is no standard answer. Whoever understands the goods or services best will usually create the first draft. Often

---

4   Most contracts have an "entire agreement" or "integration" clause, which is meant to void promises made before the contract was signed. See *Entire Agreement*, Section III.O, on page 123.

that's the provider. But sometimes a recipient drafts specs for an RFP (request for proposal) regarding customized technology, and those specs become part of the ultimate contract.

Both recipients and providers often leave specs-drafting to programmers and engineers. That's usually appropriate, but if the businesspeople responsible for the deal don't get involved, the specs may not reflect the business' goals. Let's take a contract for a customized human resources computer system. The recipient's technical folks might draft the specs because they're familiar with the technology. But it's the HR staff-members who know best what the system should do. If they're not involved, the specs won't fully address HR's needs—and neither will the system.

In other words, whoever is responsible for the deal should play a role in drafting the specs, even if that's a technically-challenged businessperson or lawyer.

That doesn't mean a businessperson or lawyer has to write specs. Much of the writing will be technical, and most of us wouldn't know where to start. If a non-tech businessperson or lawyer is responsible for the deal, he or she should go over the specs with the technical staff, to make sure they describe the desired system. And someone should edit the specs for clarity.

3. Editing Specifications

The job of drafting technical specifications lies outside the scope of this book,[5] but you should apply the lessons learned here to *edit* your specs. In other words, describe each concept as simply and clearly as possible. Limit technical jargon. And when you must use a technical term, provide a clear definition.

There is no standard length. Specs should run as long as necessary to express the business goal for the technology. Nor is there a standard organization. Specs might appear as a three-page or eighty-page list of bullet points: "The System will provide the following functionality: (1)...." Or the specs might appear as a narrative: an essay describing machine-based services or technology. If you choose the narrative, though, include paragraph numbers for ease of reference.

---

5   You can find guides on drafting technical specifications both online and in book-stores.

B. Service Level Agreements

"Service level agreement" refers to a clause or set of clauses addressing the performance of machine-based services.[1] These clauses do not usually appear in contracts for software or professional services.

Despite the name, a service level agreement ("SLA") is not generally a separate contract. It could be a separate document incorporated into the contract—maybe something attached or posted at a website. Or it could be another set of terms in the contract's main body: "Section 10: Service Level Agreement."

SLA's tell the recipient any or all of the following: (1) how provider will fix the service if it doesn't perform, (2) what kind of credit the recipient gets if the service doesn't perform and/or the provider doesn't fix it, and (3) in rare cases, what kind of extra "incentive fees" the provider gets if the service performs better than required.

This book separates service level agreements from technical specifications. Specifications say what the service will *do*, while SLA's provide remedies for failure and incentives for good performance. But some contracts mix remedies in with technical specifications. In those contracts, technical specifications and SLA's can't be divided into separate sections the way this book does—and clauses called "service level agreements" will usually include technical specifications.[2]

1. SLA Remedies

There is no required length or format for an SLA. Just express the parties' expectations regarding service remedies.

---

1   See *Promise of Machine-Based Services*, Section I.F, on page 47, for more on machine-based services.
2   See *Technical Specifications*, Section II.A, on page 53.

SLA Remedy Terms

Provider will address System faults as follows:

Level 1 Error: Response within 1 minute; Remedy within 3 hours.

Level 2 Error: Response within 3 minutes; Remedy within 12 hours.

Level 3 Error: Response within 1 hour; Remedy within 5 Business Days

As used above:

(a) "Remedy" refers to a solution that returns the System to full performance as required in the Technical Specifications.

(b) "Response" refers to an e-mail, telephone, or in-person acknowledgement of a technical support request.

(c) "Error" refers to any failure of the System to perform as required in the Technical Specifications.

(i) "Level 1 Error" refers to failure of the Security Functions.

(ii) "Level 2 Error" refers to any failure not constituting a Level 1 or Level 3 Error.

(iii) "Level 3 Error" refers to any failure not involving Security Functions, which impacts graphical user interfaces but does not prevent full data display.

—

Provider will exercise its best efforts to maintain average round-trip transmission time ("Latency") of 35 milliseconds between Key Routers ("Target Latency") at all times. In the event that average Latency exceeds Target Latency during any calendar month, Provider will credit Recipient 1% of such month's applicable service fees for each millisecond by which average Latency exceeds Target Latency; provided such credit will not exceed 40% of any month's otherwise-applicable service fees. In the event that average Latency falls below 25 milliseconds during any calendar month, Provider may invoice Recipient for incentive fees equal to 1% of that month's applicable services fee for each average millisecond below 25, up to 25% of the applicable service fees.

The key remedy is often repair. The provider promises to fix a faulty service within some set period, as in the first example in the clause box above.

Many SLA's also include credits. If the service doesn't work, or if the provider doesn't fix it fast enough, the recipient gets a credit—or in some rare cases a refund.

The credit or refund will generally be the recipient's only compensation. The recipient can't get a court to order additional payments as damages for breach.[3]

An incentive works in the opposite direction. If the service performs better than promised, the recipient has to pay extra fees, as in the second example above. Recipients should hesitate before accepting incentive terms. They're appropriate in some cases, but the recipient should ask itself whether better-than-expected performance is worth money.

2. Refunds after Termination

What happens to SLA credits if the contract expires, or if someone terminates it?

Credits after Termination

Credits issued pursuant to this SLA apply to outstanding or future invoices only and are forfeited upon termination of this Agreement. Provider is not required to issue refunds against such credits under any circumstances, including without limitation termination.

—

Provider will issue refunds against any outstanding credits issued pursuant to this Attachment B within sixty (60) days of termination of this Agreement for any reason.

SLA's generally limit remedies to credits, rather than refunds, and provide that credits disappear if the agreement terminates. See the first example in the clause box above. For the provider, that policy preserves revenues and gives customers an incentive to stick around.

Some contracts, however, do allow conversion from credits to refunds. See the second example in the clause box. Providers should consider limiting the types of termination that trigger refunds. For instance, the SLA might allow conversion for any termination "other than termination for Recipient's breach."

---

3   That's because SLA credits and refunds are generally seen as "liquidated damages," and liquidated damages are usually exclusive remedies. See *Liquidated Damages*, Section II.P, on page 104.

3. The Material Breach Issue

Many SLA's are silent on a key issue: at what point is service so bad that the recipient can terminate the contract? In other words, at what point do service level errors count as material breach of contract?

Providers generally don't want their customers terminating. But failure to address material breach in the SLA doesn't necessarily protect the provider. At some point, bad service will probably authorize the recipient to terminate, even if the contract is silent on the issue. By addressing material breach in the SLA, providers can make termination more predictable.

SLA Material Breach and Termination

In the event of ten (10) or more Level 2 or worse Errors in Recipient's system during any calendar month, Recipient may terminate this Agreement for material breach pursuant to the provisions of Section 7 (Termination), provided Recipient notifies Provider in writing of termination within fifteen (15) days of the end of such calendar month.

The example in the clause box above authorizes termination for material breach if service falls below a certain level. It also protects the provider by setting a time-limit on termination. The recipient can't terminate the contract in November because of bad service in January.

C. Warranty

A warranty promises that something is true. It's a guaranty. A warranty can cover any topic, and it can come from either the recipient or the provider, though provider warranties are more common. Providers often warrant that software or other goods will work, at least for a certain period. They also often warrant their right to transfer intellectual property. Warranty clauses may also list remedies for breach of warranty.

Warranty clauses are appropriate for most end-user software licenses. They're also appropriate for distribution agreements, if the distributor needs the sort of protections a recipient would get. Warranties are less common in services contracts, though not *un*common. (The examples below, however, all relate to software agreements.)

Warranties pack more punch than other representations. The warrantor is held more strictly to its word. It's not always clear, though, how to draw a line between warranties and garden-variety representations. The use of the term "warranty" or "warrant" helps establish warranty status, but it's not strictly necessary. In general, if one party represents a fact, and the other decides to sign the contract in reliance on that fact, the representation is probably a warranty.

1. Warranty of Function

The warranty of function promises that software will "work."

> ### *Warranty of Function*
>
> Provider warrants that, during the one year period following delivery, the Software will perform materially as described in the technical specifications set forth in Exhibit A.
>
> —
>
> Provider warrants that, during the first 180 days after installation, each New Module will perform according to its documentation issued by Provider under the heading "Official Product Documentation."

What does it mean to warrant that software or services will "work"? A clear warranty clause answers that by referring to the contract's technical specifications, as in the first example in the clause box above. In other words, the warranty says that the software will perform as required in the technical specs attached to the contract.[1]

Unfortunately, warranties of function are often much less clear. For instance: "Provider represents and warrants that the Software will be in good working order." Ugh. What does that mean? A slight improvement might read that the system will "perform according to its documentation." But what is documentation? Brochures, e-mails from salespeople, ads posted online...? If you're going to reference documentation not attached to the contract, state which documents you mean. For instance, the provider might put a label or stamp on official documentation, as in the second example above. That clause is more or less adequate, assuming the provider is careful to stamp "Official Product Documentation" in the appropriate places—and assuming there can be no doubt which documents qualify, those documents are clear, they explain what the product is supposed to do (like technical specs), and the recipient has reviewed them.

The provider can warrant just about anything in terms of functionality. Some warranties are customized and address the particular needs of the deal. For instance: "Provider warrants that no Deliverable, when installed, will impair the System's ability to process purchase and sales transactions at the speeds set forth in Exhibit C."

Providers often qualify warranties of function by requiring only "material" conformity with specs or with other requirements, as in the first example in

---

1   See *Technical Specifications*, Section II.A, on page 53.

the clause box. If every glitch counted as a breach of warranty, the provider would be in trouble. The use of "material" excludes unimportant errors.

Finally, warranties of function often have time limits, as in both examples above. If the goods stop working the day after the warranty expires (as required by Murphy's Law), the provider is off the hook. But a time limit is not required. The provider could warrant the goods indefinitely or "during the term of this Agreement."

2. Infringement/Ownership Warranty

The infringement or ownership warranty guarantees property rights, particularly rights in intellectual property. It promises that no third party will come along and keep the recipient from using the software or the rights transferred, through a claim to own them. In other words, the provider is saying, "We guarantee we have the authority to license these IP rights." Infringement warranties are appropriate for nearly all software contracts.

> *Infringement Warranty*
>
> Provider warrants that it is the owner of the System and of each and every component thereof, or the recipient of a valid license thereto, and that it has obtained and will maintain the full power and authority to grant the rights granted in this Agreement without the further consent of any person or entity.

Some providers balk at the IP side of this clause: "How can we guarantee that? There are millions of patents, covering all kinds of technologies. How can we possibly be sure our product doesn't infringe one of them?" The answer is that the provider *can't* be sure. Nor can most providers be sure their engineers didn't illegally copy a few lines of code. But providers don't need to be sure because this warranty isn't about certainty. It's about *allocation of risk*. The warranty provides that the provider, not the recipient, bears the legal risk that the goods infringe some third party's IP. That's usually appropriate because it's *the provider's* product. The provider is in a better position to create safeguards: to do a patent search, to hire engineers who are honest and careful, etc.

That's not to say the provider has to accept that risk. If the provider has leverage, it can refuse to guarantee IP rights or general ownership rights.

3. Other Warranties

Warranties can cover almost any topic. The examples in the clause box below are common, but you should craft whatever language fits your deal.

Special Warranties

Each party warrants that it has the full right and authority to enter into, execute, and perform its obligations under this Agreement and that no pending or threatened claim or litigation would have a material adverse impact on such party's ability to perform as required by this Agreement.

—

Provider represents and warrants that the Software and any media used to distribute it contain no viruses or other computer instructions or technological means whose purpose is to disrupt, damage, or interfere with the use of computers or related systems.

—

Provider warrants that the Licensed Program does not include software subject to any legal requirement that would restrict Distributor's right to distribute the Licensed Program, or any modification thereof: (a) for a fee, (b) with or without source code or source code rights, and (c) with such restrictions as Distributor sees fit to place on its customers' modification, distribution, and other rights.

—

Provider warrants that all Services will be performed in a workmanlike manner.

—

Provider warrants that the Services will comply with all applicable laws, including without limitation federal, state, and local.

The third example in the clause box protects software distributors against open source software provided with a "copyleft" or "viral" license.[2] The fourth promises that services will be "workmanlike": a somewhat vague but common term meaning professional and skilled. The others should be self-explanatory.

---

2   See *Software Licenses in General, Open Source License*, Subsection I.C.4, on page 29.

Remember that warranties don't truly promise a state of affairs. Rather, *they shift legal risk.* So the provider might not actually be able to guarantee that it won't deliver a computer virus, or that its services comply with every conceivable law—as in the second and last examples above. But the provider can promise to take the blame for a virus or a broken law or anything else. It can accept the legal risk.

4. Exclusion of Warranties

Many providers use the warranty clause primarily to *disclaim* warranties.

Warranty Exclusions

EXCEPT FOR THE EXPRESS WARRANTIES SPECIFIED IN THIS SECTION, PROVIDER MAKES NO WARRANTIES, EITHER EXPRESS OR IMPLIED, INCLUDING WITHOUT LIMITATION ANY IMPLIED WARRANTY OF MERCHANTABILITY OR FITNESS FOR A PARTICULAR PURPOSE.

—

RECIPIENT ACCEPTS THE GOODS "AS IS," WITH NO REPRESENTATION OR WARRANTY OF ANY KIND, EXPRESS OR IMPLIED, INCLUDING WITHOUT LIMITATION IMPLIED WARRANTIES OF MERCHANTABILITY OR FITNESS FOR A PARTICULAR PURPOSE.

—

Provider does not warrant that the Product will perform without error or that it will run without immaterial interruption. Provider provides no warranty regarding, and will have no responsibility for, any claim arising out of: (a) a modification made by Recipient, unless Provider approves such modification in writing; or (b) use of the Product in combination with or on products other than as specified in the Technical Specifications or authorized in writing by Provider.

—

> Provider: (a) will pass through to Recipient any warranty right it receives from any third party provider of System components not authored or manufactured by Provider ("Third Party Components"); and (b) will reasonably cooperate with Recipient in enforcing such rights. Provider provides no warranties, express or implied, with regard to Third Party Components, and Provider will not be liable for any failure of any Third Party Component to function as expected or intended.

The vast majority of software and services contracts include a disclaimer of *implied* warranties, like the first example in the clause box above. The laws of most states impose certain warranties on sales contracts, even if those warranties are not actually written down. The two of greatest concern are the *implied warranty of merchantability* and the *implied warranty of fitness for a particular purpose*. "Merchantability" warrants, among other things, that the goods will do what they're supposed to do: they are fit for their ordinary purposes. That makes sense for cars and toasters, because everyone knows what they do. But software and IT services have many complex functions, and reasonable minds can differ about their ordinary purposes. So providers almost always disclaim the implied warranty of merchantability.

"Fitness for a particular purpose" warrants that a product will be appropriate for the recipient's unique needs. In the IT business, the provider often doesn't fully understand the recipient's needs, or know them at all. So providers specifically disclaim the implied warranty of fitness for a particular purpose.

Disclaimers of implied warranties are appropriate for both software and services contracts.[3] Courts are often receptive to arguments that the recipient didn't understand the clause's importance (particularly if the recipient is a consumer). So the disclaimer should be conspicuous, appearing in all caps.

Another common disclaimer relates to misuse of the Software. If the recipient modifies the software and that leads to a malfunction or a third party suit, the provider is not responsible. The same goes for the recipient's use of the software on an unauthorized platform. See the third example in the clause box above.

---

3 Technically speaking, the disclaimer isn't necessary for services contracts, because most states' laws don't impose implied warranties on them. But the line between goods and services can be hazy in IT, so it's best to include the disclaimer anyway.

   In some states, it's harder to enforce a disclaimer, or an "as is" warranty, than in others.

Still another common disclaimer relates to third party components. A provider might design and sell a computer system that includes hardware and software from third parties, as well as its own software. Since the provider didn't produce the third party components, it might not be able to trust them. Worse, the third parties might have given the provider a weak warranty, or none. So the provider could find itself on the hook alone. The solution is to pass through any third party warranties to the recipient and disclaim any other warranty on third party components, as in the last example in the clause box above.

Of course, this sort of pass-through causes problems for the recipient. If the system doesn't work, the provider and third party manufacturer will likely blame each other. That's why many recipients argue that, if the provider *resells* the third party component, it should take responsibility for it. Otherwise, why doesn't the recipient purchase directly from the third party—for less, without the provider's mark-up? Recipients also argue that the whole reason for hiring a single technology integrator (the provider) is to get a single point of contact: a single party responsible for the system. As with all contract negotiations, the resolution comes down to leverage: who needs the deal more?

Finally, providers often disclaim specific issues in the warranty clause. For instance: "Provider does not warrant the Software's interoperability with any computer operating system other than the versions of Windows XP issued by Microsoft Corporation as of the Effective Date." Craft whatever disclaimers fit your deal.

5. Remedies for Breach of Warranty

A contract doesn't have to specify a remedy for breach of warranty. If it doesn't, a court will impose money damages or other solutions. But by agreeing on the remedies in advance, the parties remove much of the element of chance.

Remedies for Breach of Warranty

In the event of breach of the warranty set forth in this Section, Provider will promptly repair or replace the Product in question, or if such attempts do not succeed after sixty (60) days of reasonable effort, refund all amounts paid by Recipient for such Product. The preceding sentence states Recipient's sole remedy, and Provider's entire liability, for breach of such warranty.

—

> If the Software becomes, or in either party's reasonable opinion is likely to become, the subject of any claim, suit, or proceeding arising from or alleging infringement of any intellectual property right, or in the event of any adjudication that the Software infringes on any such right, Provider, at its own expense, will promptly take the following actions: (a) secure for Recipient the right to continue using the Software, or if that effort fails; (b) replace or modify the Software to make it noninfringing, provided that such modification or replacement will not render the Software non-compliant with its Technical Specifications. The remedies set forth in the preceding sentence are not exclusive of any others Recipient may have at law or in equity.

Usually, the provider promises to repair or replace defective goods, as in the first example in the clause box above. And for infringement warranties, the provider promises it will get the recipient a license to keep using the goods, or replace them with something non-infringing, as in the second example.

But what if these strategies fail? What if the thing can't be fixed, or the provider can't afford a license and there's no suitable replacement? For the provider, the best solution is often to refund the recipient's money, take the product back, and walk away. The first example in the clause box gives the provider that right.

The refund and walk away solution may leave the recipient in the lurch. Imagine the product is an accounting computer system, and the recipient's already thrown away the old system. If the recipient has to stop using the new one, it has nothing, and it's in trouble—trouble a refund won't solve. That's why recipients prefer clauses like the second example in the clause box, which leaves the provider no way out other than *fix or replace*. That should motivate the provider to go the extra mile looking for a solution (or at least drag the provider down with the recipient).[4]

If the contract specifies remedies for breach of warranty, will those remedies be "exclusive"? In other words, once the provider has repaired or replaced the product, can the recipient still go after money damages or some other remedy? If the contract says nothing on the subject, there's a good chance the recipient can. To make sure, recipients often include clauses like the last sen-

---

4   Of course, if the contract has a strong limitation of liability clause, the provider still might not be very motivated to help. See *Limitation of Liability*, Section II.G, on page 78.

tence in the second example above, providing that these remedies are not "exclusive." The provider, of course, wants to limit its responsibility to the stated remedies. So the first example in the clause box provides that the remedies *are* exclusive.

D. Schedule and Milestones

Some services need a schedule or an end-date. For example, at some point in a technology development project, the computer system has to be designed, built, and ready for use. Those deadlines appear in a scheduling clause.

Schedule of Services

Provider will complete the Project on or before February 12, 2008.

—

Section 5. Milestones

Provider will complete the Service by the following deadlines ("Milestones"):

A. Alpha Version operational: 90 days after Effective Date;

B. Beta Version operational: 130 days after Effective Date;

C. System complete and submitted for Acceptance Testing: 175 days after Effective Date

Section 6. Payment

Recipient will pay Provider in the following installments:

*   Milestone A: 30% of the Contract Fee

*   Milestone B: 30% of the Contract Fee

*   Milestone C: 10% of the Contract Fee

*   Successful completion of Acceptance Testing: 30% of the Contract Fee

---

The simplest way to handle scheduling is to provide a deadline for completion of the project, as in the first example in the clause box above. But for a long or complex project, you often need several deadlines, or milestones. See the second example above.[1]

Milestones can serve as powerful incentives if they're linked to the recipient's payment obligations, as in the second example. The provider will perform much more quickly if it gets paid at each important step along the way—an obvious benefit for the recipient. And for the provider, a milestones payment structure may be the only way to get some of the fee before finishing the job.

A source of dispute hangs over all scheduling clauses. *What if the provider needs the recipient's cooperation to finish on time, and the recipient doesn't cooperate?* What if the provider needs instructions from the recipient, or equipment, or access to the building—and the recipient takes forever? The provider shouldn't be held responsible for the delay. Sometime you can handle this issue through a lockstep scheduling clause: "Recipient will provide an instructions memo by June 9. Provider will complete Phase 1 within thirty days of receiving the instructions memo...." That way, the clock doesn't start ticking on the provider's performance until after the recipient cooperates.

But often the recipient's task is not easily defined. Often the provider needs general and miscellaneous cooperation: a million small favors that will make the project run smoothly. This is one of the hardest problems to address in a contract. One solution is to provide extra time to complete each milestone, so that if the recipient fails to cooperate, the provider can still get done on time. Another is to include something like: "All deadlines are subject to such extension as is reasonably necessary if Recipient does not cooperate in good faith with Provider, including by providing the following forms of assistance: ...." The problem, of course, is that terms like "cooperate," "good faith," and "reasonably necessary" are vague. Try to draft the scheduling clause as clearly as possible, but recognize that you may have to accept some of these wiggle words.

At some point, the recipient's failure to cooperate crosses over into breach or termination of contract. For that issue, see *Sale of Professional Services, Change Orders and Midstream Terminations*, Subsection I.E.2, on page 41.

---

1   One of the deadlines might be completion of acceptance testing, as in the second example in the clause box above. For acceptance testing, see *Delivery, Acceptance, and Rejection*, Section II.E, on page 72.

E. Delivery, Acceptance, and Rejection

Delivery, acceptance, and rejection clauses are appropriate for many software licenses and some assignments and work-for-hire agreements. At their simplest, they provide instructions for the provider about the time and place of computer and software delivery. But some clauses go further and call for "acceptance tests." The recipient can test the software to make sure it works. If the software fails, the recipient can reject it, and the provider usually has to fix it or refund the money.

Delivery, Acceptance, & Rejection

Provider will deliver one copy of the Software, in compact disk format, to Recipient's facility at 325 Chestnut Avenue, Mobile, Alabama, 36601 within sixty (60) days of the Effective Date.

———

Provider will install the System in Recipient's Juneau Facility on or before ninety (90) days after the Effective Date ("Delivery"). Upon Delivery, Recipient may perform such tests as it sees fit to determine whether the System conforms to its Specifications. The System will be considered accepted: (a) when Recipient provides Provider written notice of acceptance, or (b) thirty (30) days after Delivery, if Recipient has not first provided Provider with written notice of rejection (collectively, "Acceptance"). Recipient may reject the System only in the event that it materially deviates from the Specifications. In the event of such rejection, Provider will, at its option, (i) repair the System and re-deliver it within fifteen (15) days, or (ii) take back the System and refund all amounts paid pursuant to this Agreement. Re-delivery pursuant to the previous sentence will be considered

> another Delivery, and the parties will again follow the acceptance procedures set forth in this Section 5, except that in the event of a second rejection, Recipient may elect to terminate this Agreement, return the System, and receive a full refund of all amounts paid pursuant to this Agreement. The refunds and other remedies authorized by this Section are not exclusive of any other remedies Recipient may have.

The first example in the clause box above is a simple delivery provision. The second is an acceptance clause.

Acceptance testing is most common for customized software: systems the provider creates or modifies to fit the recipient's needs. But contracts for more standard goods can include acceptance tests too, if the recipient has enough leverage.

The provider should not give the recipient freedom to reject goods for any old reason, or because they don't meet expectations the recipient never mentioned. The clearest test provides that the goods fail if they don't conform to their technical specifications, as in the second example in the clause box.[1] But some contracts lay out much narrower tests, defining steps the recipient can take to test the goods. "The Software will be considered accepted only if it passes all three Tests listed on Attachment B."

One risk for the provider is that the recipient will never get around to testing the goods, or will take a long time. That's particularly troubling if the provider doesn't get *paid* until acceptance. That's why many acceptance clauses have a "deemed acceptance" provision, as in the second example in the clause box. If the recipient doesn't either accept or reject within X days, the goods are *deemed* accepted.

What if the goods fail the test? The contract might require that the provider fix them or refund the recipient's money, as in the second example above.

If the provider tries to fix the goods and redelivers them, the parties could find themselves going around the same rejection, fix, and redelivery loop indefinitely. So an important issue is: who decides when to give up and recognize that the goods won't work? In the second example above, the provider can give up and go home after the first rejection. After that, either party can make that decision.

Some contracts add another remedy for goods that don't pass the test on time: late fees. The provider usually pays late fees through a credit or partial refund: "In the event of Rejection, Provider will credit Recipient 1% of the

---

1   See *Technical Specifications*, Section II.A, on page 53.

License Fee for every Business Day until the delivery date of Software that passes the Acceptance Tests." If you use late fees, review *Liquidated Damages*, Section II.P, on page 104.

Finally, the contract should state whether the recipient's remedy for failure of acceptance tests—and for any related delay—is exclusive. Providers, of course, prefer terms saying the recipient's remedies *are* exclusive. "The remedies set forth in this Section 5 are Recipient's sole remedies for failure of Acceptance Tests." In other words, once the provider has fixed the goods or refunded the money, it's off the hook. It isn't liable for breach of contract damages. Recipients, on the other hand, generally prefer language saying the contract remedies are not exclusive, as in the second example in the clause box above.

F. Indemnity

In an indemnity clause, one party promises to protect the other from some bad event—to the cover the other party's losses. The responsible party, the "indemnitor," could be the recipient or the provider. Indemnity clauses are appropriate for all kinds of software and services contracts.

The clause should specify the event or events that trigger the payment obligation. Usually, it's something the indemnitor might cause. For instance, if the indemnitor sells software that infringes someone's IP rights, and gets the recipient sued, the indemnitor will pay the damages. The clause might also specify the *types* of losses the indemnitor will cover: compensation for property damages, attorneys' fees, lawsuit judgments, etc.

Some IT contracts include very broad indemnity obligations: "Each party will indemnify the other against any losses caused by such other party's negligence or breach of this contract." In most relationships, that's overkill. Indemnity should cover losses that particularly concern one party or the other. In software and services, the most common risks relate to third party suits against the recipient, triggered by the provider's actions or omissions. So the provider is usually the indemnitor.

Indemnity

Provider will indemnify, defend, settle at its expense, and hold Recipient harmless from any third party claim, suit, or proceeding claiming that the Software infringes intellectual property rights. Notwithstanding the foregoing, such indemnity obligation will not apply to claims, suits, or proceedings arising out of: (a) revisions to the Software made by Recipient without Provider's advanced written consent and which caused the alleged infringement; or (b) Recipient's failure to incorporate free Software updates or upgrades from Provider that would have avoided the alleged infringement.

> Provider will defend, settle at its expense, and pay any judgment arising out of any third party claim, suit, or proceeding against Recipient or any of its officers, directors, parents, subsidiaries, agents, insurers, successors, assigns, stockholders, or attorneys arising out of, related to, or alleging: (i) the injury to or death of any individual, or any loss or damage to real or tangible personal property, caused by the negligence of Provider or any of its agents, subcontractors, or employees; or (ii) infringement of any patent, copyright, or other intellectual property right by the System (collectively, the "Covered Claims"). Recipient will give Provider prompt notice of, and Provider will control the defense of, any Covered Claim, including appeals, negotiations, and any settlement or compromise thereof; provided that Recipient will have the right to approve the terms of any settlement or compromise that restricts its rights granted under this Agreement or subjects it to any ongoing obligations.

Usually, the contract requires that the indemnitor defend the other party against any covered claim and pay any judgments or settlements. Both examples in the clause box promise just that. But the first example—like most technology contracts—uses several slightly redundant terms to express that obligation. It includes two terms left out of the second example: "hold harmless" and the word "indemnify" itself. The two have similar and loosely defined legal meanings. Arguably, "indemnify" and "hold harmless" demand more than just payment of lawyers, judgments, and settlements. Arguably, they require that the indemnitor reimburse any loss, including loss of business. Some technology providers won't risk such a broad obligation and leave the two terms out. Those providers simply promise to defend the case and pay any settlement or judgment, as in the second example. (But we'll still use the terms "indemnitor" and "indemnity" regarding these clauses.)

The most common covered claim is an IP suit against the recipient—addressed in both examples in the clause box above. Imagine the provider provides software that illegally uses a third party's patented technology. It's probably an innocent mistake, but that doesn't help the recipient. The third party sues the recipient. The recipient might have to stop using the software.

And it might be liable for damages. The provider's product creates this risk, so the provider promises to protect the recipient.[1]

Usually, the indemnity promises protection from all covered claims, even meritless ones. If someone sues the recipient, even on the most ridiculous claim, the provider will pay the costs. That's how both examples work in the clause box above.

Sometimes, the provider protects itself by clarifying that indemnification duties end if the recipient modifies the technology and causes the infringement that way, or fails to install a free update that would have avoided the problem. See the first example in the clause box.

Some indemnity clauses address suits about personal injuries or property damage, but that's less common. In the second example in the clause box above, the concern is that, while providing services to the recipient or delivering goods, the provider's employees will drop a crate on someone's foot, or sexually harass someone, or compromise someone's personal data, or burn down a building. The injured party sues everyone, including the innocent recipient. Often, providers aren't willing to take responsibility for these types of suits. But if the provider does accept such a clause, it should try to limit the indemnity to suits caused by negligence, rather than innocent mistake on the one hand, or employees who go crazy and do intentional harm on the other. See the second example above.[2]

Often, indemnity clauses require that the recipient give the provider prompt notice of the claim and let the provider run the defense. And some clauses give the recipient authority to approve any settlement, or at least any settlement that restricts its rights. See the second example in the clause box above.

---

1   An IP indemnity covers the same ground as an IP warranty, so some of the same considerations apply. As with IP warranties, the provider can never be entirely sure the software doesn't infringe third party rights. Providers often accept indemnity clauses anyway to shift the risk. It's the provider's product, so the provider will protect the recipient. For more on this issue, see *Warranty, Infringement/Ownership Warranty*, Subsection II.C.2, on page 63.

2   The contract's limitation of liability clause may also limit the provider's obligations. See *Limitation of Liability*, Section II.G, on page 78.

G. Limitation of Liability

Limitation of liability clauses appear in almost all software and services contracts. They usually protect the provider, but sometimes they protect both parties.

To newcomers, the limitation of liability often seems bizarre. The clause says that if one party injures the other, it's not responsible for the full damages. Imagine the provider supplies defective software. The software malfunctions, and as a result, the recipient loses a million dollars—due to missed opportunities, mismanaged assets, costs of finding replacement software, etc. Imagine also that the limitation of liability clause caps the provider's liability at $50,000. The result: the provider is liable for *one twentieth* of the recipient's loss. Even if everyone agrees the malfunction was the provider's fault—and foreseeable—the provider owes $50K, and that's all.

What recipient would agree to such a thing, and why? The answer is, *almost every recipient*, and there's a good reason why.

The feature of IT that makes the industry so profitable makes limitation of liability clauses standard. That feature is *scalability*. Information technology is an unusually scalable tool: it can be used to achieve goals many times more valuable than the tool itself. You can use a five thousand dollar software program to design a half-billion dollar bridge. You can use a ten thousand dollar computer to manage a billion dollar asset portfolio. And that same low-cost software application or computer can single-handedly *ruin* a half-billion dollar bridge or a billion dollar asset portfolio.

If the provider faced potential liability of a billion dollars, or even a half million dollars, with every $5,000 sale, it couldn't do business. One malfunction could wipe out ten years of profits. That's why software and IT services providers insist on limitations of liability.

Often, software and services contracts also limit the recipient's liability. The usual recipient rationale is: "If your liability's limited, so is ours." Some providers don't accept that logic, but some do. That's why many limitation of liability clauses protect both parties. However, because it's the provider that faces the most liability, it's usually the provider that pushes for a strong clause.

Limitation of liability clauses come in two common flavors: dollar caps and exclusions of consequential damages. Most contracts feature both, as overlapping protections. Many limitation clauses also have exceptions: types of liability that are *not* limited. We will address each of these in turn.

1. Dollar Cap

The simplest part of the limitation of liability clause caps the parties' liability at a dollar figure.

Dollar Cap Limitation of Liability

PROVIDER'S LIABILITY ARISING OUT OF OR RELATED TO THIS AGREEMENT, INCLUDING WITHOUT LIMITATION LIABILITY FOR NEGLIGENCE, WILL NOT EXCEED $50,000.

—

NEITHER PARTY'S LIABILITY TO THE OTHER ARISING OUT OF OR RELATED TO THIS AGREEMENT WILL EXCEED THE ANNUAL LICENSE FEE. LIABILITIES LIMITED BY THE PRECEDING SENTENCE INCLUDE, WITHOUT LIMITATION, LIABILITY FOR NEGLIGENCE.

The dollar cap could be a million or five thousand or anything else. Often the figure isn't set ahead of time. Instead, it's calculated through some formula, as in the second example in the clause box above.

The dollar cap is somewhat arbitrary. You can pick any figure or any way of calculating a figure. Providers often forget this and complain that a high dollar cap isn't "fair." The size of the dollar cap depends on leverage, not fairness. In other words, which party wants the deal most, and what risks can the parties accept? (So risk-management policies should play a role in picking a figure, along with the demands of insurance carriers—particularly the provider's insurers.)

The clause should clarify that it caps liability for negligence. Some courts won't enforce a cap on negligence liability unless it's explicit. And courts often won't enforce a cap if they think the recipient didn't understand its importance (particularly if the recipient is a consumer). So the clause should stand out, appearing in capital letters. See both examples in the clause box above.

2. Exclusion of Consequential Damages

The exclusion of consequential damages focuses on the *type* of liability, not the dollar amount. (The clause may exclude "indirect," "special," "punitive," and various other types of damages. All of those but punitive—discussed below—are flavors of consequential damages.)

> *Exclusion of Consequential Damages*
>
> IN NO EVENT WILL EITHER PARTY BE LIABLE TO THE OTHER FOR ANY CONSEQUENTIAL, INDIRECT, SPECIAL, INCIDENTAL, OR PUNITIVE DAMAGES, REGARDLESS OF THE FORM OF ACTION, WHETHER IN CONTRACT, TORT (INCLUDING WITHOUT LIMITATION NEGLIGENCE), STRICT PRODUCT LIABILITY, OR OTHERWISE, EVEN IF ADVISED IN ADVANCE OF THE POSSIBILITY OF SUCH DAMAGES AND EVEN IF SUCH DAMAGES WERE FORESEEABLE.

To understand consequential damages, let's return to our example of a software application used to design a bridge. The software malfunctions, and as a result, the bridge is defective and falls apart. The recipient designed the bridge and owns it, and it wants two kinds of compensation from the software provider: direct and consequential damages. The *direct* damage is the cost of replacing the software, as well as various related expenses, probably pretty modest. The *consequential* damage is the price tag on all the unique consequences of this particular failure: the cost of repairing or replacing the bridge, the cost of paying off any injured drivers or pedestrians, loss of the recipient's time, loss of other business opportunities, loss of reputation, etc. In this case, the direct damages might be about $15,000: mostly the price of new software. The consequential damages could total millions or billions.[1]

Consequential damages are unpredictable and theoretically unlimited (though some state laws impose limits). That's why software and services vendors generally insist on limiting them.

Obviously, a dollar cap would also prevent liability for much of the money at stake in a consequential damages claim. The two clauses overlap.

---

1   More specifically, direct damages are losses anyone in the recipient's position might suffer. Consequential damages are consequences of *this* recipient's unique situation. Since not everyone using the software designs a billion-dollar bridge, the billion dollar loss would usually count as consequential damages. But the line between direct and consequential damages depends on the context, and it's not always clear. In some cases, direct damages are very high.

Some states won't fully enforce an exclusion of consequential damages. So the clause might provide: "If applicable law limits the application of the provisions of the preceding sentence, Provider's liability will be limited to the maximum extent permissible." Also, as with dollar caps, limits on consequential damages should specifically mention liability for negligence and should appear in capital letters, to maximize chances of full enforcement. See the example in the clause box above.

Limitation of liability clauses sometimes exclude punitive damages. Punitive damages go beyond compensation and punish someone who's done wrong. They're usually not available in contract cases. But the law is not always predictable, and there's no harm in throwing "punitive" into the list with "consequential," "special," etc., as in the example above.

3. Exceptions: Liability That's Not Limited

The parties often agree that the clause will not limit certain forms of liability.

> *Exceptions to Limitation of Liability*
>
> The limitations of this Section 8 do not apply to: (a) claims arising out of or related to breach of the warranty in Section 10(b) (IP Infringement) or to any other infringement of third party intellectual property rights by Provider; (b) claims pursuant to any provision of this Agreement calling for liquidated damages; (c) claims pursuant to Section 8 (Indemnity); or (d) claims for attorneys' fees and other litigation costs either party becomes entitled to recover as a prevailing party in any action.
>
> —
>
> The limitations of liability in this Section 8 do not apply to any claims of infringement of Provider's intellectual property, including without limitation copyrights in the Software.

Generally, the exceptions carve out liabilities created by the contract itself. The most common such exceptions are for liquidated damages, for indemnity, and for breach of an intellectual property warranty—all addressed in the first example in the clause box.[2]

---

2   See *Liquidated Damages*, Section II.P, on page 104; *Indemnity*, Section II.F, on page 75; and *Warranty, Infringement/Ownership Warranty*, Subsection II.C.2, on page 63.

Software providers should consider another exception—but only where the limitation of liability clause protects the recipient (rather than just the provider). What if the recipient infringes the provider's copyright by creating too many copies of the software? What if, instead of creating two copies, as authorized in the license section, the recipient creates 10,000? If the limitation of liability clause caps damages at the contract price, the recipient arguably gets 10,000 for the price of two. Of course, a court might not stand for such contract-assisted theft, but the provider shouldn't take the risk. That's why the second example in the clause box above carves out liability for IP infringement by the recipient.

Providers granting mutual clauses should peruse the contract for other liabilities that should *not* be limited. Is there some recipient promise that, if broken, would trigger large consequential damages, or otherwise lead to losses higher than the cap? Breach of a government restricted rights clause might cost the provider a fortune, for instance. So the provider might want terms saying: "The limitations of liability of this Section 8 do not apply to breach of the provisions of Subsection 14(d) (Government Restricted Rights)."[3] In general, providers should consider the limitation of liability clause *their* shield. If the protection extends to the recipient too, the provider should think through the risks and create exceptions for any it can't accept.

---

3   See *Government Restricted Rights*, Section III.G, on page 119.

H. Confidentiality / Nondisclosure

In a confidentiality clause, the parties commit to protect each other's trade secrets and other sensitive information. Such a clause can appear in almost any software or services agreement. It can also serve as the central clause in a separate nondisclosure agreement, or "NDA."

A confidentiality clause may operate in both directions or only one. In a one-way clause, only one party will disclose confidential data, and the other will receive it. In a two-way or "mutual" clause, either party may disclose or receive confidential information. Usually, such a clause calls the parties "Discloser" and "Receiver," or something like that.[1] Those names aren't attached to one party but rather rotate, depending on who's doing what. This section uses them the same way.

The examples in this section are two-way clauses. If you would like to use them for a one-way clause, delete the definitions of "Discloser" and "Receiver" in the first clause box below. Then, throughout the clause, replace those terms with whatever names you're using for your contracting parties—"Provider," "Distributor," etc.

1. What's Confidential?

Many clauses define "Confidential Information" as "any nonpublic, sensitive, or private information disclosed by the Discloser." That's generally a bad idea because there's so much room for dispute about what is "sensitive or private."

---

1   "Recipient" sounds better than "receiver," but don't use it if you're already using it for one of the parties' names.

> ### *Confidential Information Definition*
>
> "Confidential Information" refers to the following items one party to this Agreement (the "Discloser") discloses to the other party (the "Receiver"): (i) any document the Discloser marks "Confidential"; (ii) any information the Discloser orally designates as "Confidential" at the time of disclosure, provided the Discloser confirms such designation in writing within five (5) business days; and (iii) any source code for the Software disclosed by Provider, whether or not marked as confidential. Notwithstanding the foregoing, Confidential Information does not include information that: (A) is in the Receiver's possession at the time of disclosure; (B) is independently developed by the Receiver without use of or reference to Confidential Information; (C) becomes known publicly, before or after disclosure, other than as a result of the Receiver's improper action or inaction; or (D) is approved for release in writing by the Discloser.

The clearest clauses require that the discloser *mark* sensitive documents "Confidential," as in subsection (i) in the clause box above. In many contracts, that's enough. (But then the discloser has to *do* the actual marking.) In some relationships, however, confidential information will be disclosed orally: "OK, what I'm gonna tell you next is confidential, per the NDA." Because memories are not reliable, the clause should require that the discloser quickly confirm the designation in writing, as in Subsection (ii).[2]

The other way to designate confidential information is to "pre-mark" it: to identify certain types of sensitive data in advance, in the contract. Subsection

---

2   Note that any clause that lets the discloser decide what's confidential creates a risk for the receiver. The discloser could designate too much. It could disclose confidential information the receiver doesn't want—information that will be hard to protect, or that might restrict the receiver's business. If this risk is high (e.g., because of low trust), the parties can agree in advance on the information to be confidential, per the next paragraph above. Or if that's not practical, the clause could include a safety valve: "Before disclosure, the Discloser will provide the Receiver with a non-confidential written summary of any data intended to be Confidential Information. Within five (5) business days of receipt of such a summary, the Receiver may reject the information in writing. Any information disclosed without such a summary, or after such rejection, will not be considered Confidential Information."

(iii) in the clause box pre-marks source code. The key, as always, is clarity: leave no doubt as to what information is confidential.

Whatever the definition of confidential information, some data should be excluded. The example above excludes the key types: data the receiver already has or develops independently, and data in the public domain.

2. Restrictions on Use

The core terms of a confidentiality clause tell the receiver what *not* to do with confidential information. There are many ways to put it, but in short, the receiver can't pass the information on to third parties without permission.

> *Nondisclosure*
>
> The Receiver will not use the Confidential Information for any purpose other than to facilitate the transactions contemplated by this Agreement (the "Purpose"). The Receiver will not: (i) disclose Confidential Information to any employee or contractor of the Receiver unless such person needs access in order to facilitate the Purpose and executes a nondisclosure agreement with the Receiver, with terms no less restrictive than those of this Section 9; or (ii) disclose any Confidential Information to any other third party without the Discloser's prior written consent. Without limiting the generality of the foregoing,[3] the Receiver will protect the Confidential Information with the same degree of care it uses to protect its own confidential information of similar nature and importance, but no less than reasonable care. The Receiver will notify the Discloser in writing of any misuse or misappropriation of Confidential Information that comes to the Receiver's attention. Notwithstanding the foregoing, the Receiver may disclose Confidential Information as required by applicable law or by proper legal or governmental authority. In such case, the Receiver will give the Discloser advanced notice reasonably sufficient to allow the Discloser to seek a protective order or otherwise to contest such required disclosure, and will reasonably cooperate in such effort, at the Discloser's expense.

The first two sentences in the clause box lay out a "strict liability" rule: the receiver has breached the contract if it circulates the information, even accidentally. An alternative rule would require that the receiver exercise "best efforts" or "the same degree of care that it exercises to protect its own confidential information of similar nature." That sets a lesser standard. If confiden-

---

3   For an explanation of this phrase, see the footnote on page 14.

tial information gets out, but the receiver really tried to keep it safe, it hasn't breached the contract.

Note that some clauses—like the example in the clause box—impose a strict liability rule and then *also* require "reasonable efforts": slightly redundant, double-barreled protection.

Some clauses go beyond simple rules on data protection and regulate the receiver's *employees* (and independent contractors). Provisions like Subsection (i) in the clause box above allow access only on a need-to-know basis, and require that each employee sign a separate NDA. Of course, this can be burdensome for the receiver.

Another type of restriction says what the receiver *can* do with confidential information, and forbids any other use. The contract defines the *reason* for sharing confidential information: e.g., "to facilitate discussion of a business transaction between the parties." Then it provides that the receiver may use the confidential information for that purpose, and not for anything else. See the first two sentences of the example in the clause box above.

You can customize more restrictive provisions. For instance, the clause could read: "The Receiver will not make any copies of any document containing Confidential Information and will keep all such documents in a locked safe at the receiver's corporate headquarters, with keys or combinations available only to the Receiver's president."

Finally, most confidentiality clauses—including the example in the clause box above—allow the receiver to share confidential information with the police or the government, if required by law.

3. Injunction Remedy

Often, if the receiver leaks the confidential information or threatens to leak it, the discloser wants to plug the leak before it's too late. The discloser needs a court order or "injunction" directing the receiver to protect the information.

Injunctive Relief

The Receiver agrees that violation of the provisions of this Section might cause the Discloser irreparable injury, for which monetary damages would not provide adequate compensation, and that in addition to any other remedies available, the Discloser will be entitled to injunctive relief against such breach or threatened breach, without the necessity of proving actual damages.

If the contract doesn't address this injunction issue, and the parties wind up in court, the receiver could argue that the discloser doesn't really need an injunction—that money damages, granted after a trial, would be enough to compensate the discloser. To defeat that argument, the example in the clause box has the receiver admit in advance that money damages would not do the trick. The leak would injure the discloser's business in a way that no amount of money could compensate.

4. Termination and Return

Keeping secrets can be burdensome, and most secrets grow less sensitive over time. So confidentiality clauses usually fix an end date for the receiver's obligations. In a year, five years, or whenever, the receiver is off the hook.

Termination and Certification

The obligations of Subsection 9(b) above (Nondisclosure) will terminate three (3) years after disclosure of the item of Confidential Information in question. Upon termination of this Agreement, or upon the Discloser's written request, the Receiver will return all Confidential Information to the Discloser and certify, in writing, the destruction of any copies thereof.

Whenever the obligations terminate, the discloser should consider terms like the last sentence in the clause box. It requires return or destruction of confidential documents.

I. Technology Escrow

Software recipients often receive object code but not source code.[1] In many cases, the result is that the recipient won't be able to maintain or improve the software, since the technicians need source code to see how the system is supposed to work. That's not a problem if the provider offers any necessary service. But what if the provider goes out of business? Or what if the provider breaches its service obligations? If the system's vital, the recipient will be in trouble. That's why software licenses often include technology escrow provisions. (Escrows can also appear in software distribution agreements, but it's less common.)

Technology escrows can cover assets other than source code, but we will focus on source code because it's the most common.

In an escrow clause, the provider gives a reliable third party a copy of its source code, and of any supporting documentation. This third party, the "escrow agent," holds the materials for the recipient's benefit. The recipient gets the source code if an agreed "release condition" takes place. Release conditions usually include bankruptcy by the provider and breach of the provider's service obligations.

The escrow agent is necessary because the recipient can't assume it will get the source code from the provider, if and when the time comes. If the provider some-day breaches its service obligations, it might also breach any promise to turn over source code. Also, if the provider goes bankrupt, the law will probably relieve it of many contract obligations, like promises to turn over source code.

The escrow agent could be almost anyone the parties trust, but the most reliable services come from companies that specialize in technology escrows.[2] These

---

1   See the footnote on page 12 for definitions of these terms.
2   Many businesses ask one of the parties' lawyers to serve as escrow agent. That's a bad idea because it creates a conflict of interest. A lawyer should be loyal to his or her client, while an escrow agent should be neutral. Also, most law firms couldn't provide the verification services described in Subsection 1.

   Footnote continued on next page.

professional escrow agents generally have their own form contract setting up the relationship. This "escrow agreement" becomes an attachment to the parties' license agreement. Recipient, provider, and escrow agent all sign it—usually at the same time as the recipient and provider sign the license agreement.

Separate Escrow Agreement

(a) *Escrow Agreement.* Concurrent with execution of this Agreement, the parties will execute a Third Party Escrow Agreement in the form attached hereto as Attachment B ("the Escrow Agreement"), in conjunction with TechCitadel, Inc. (the "Escrow Agent").

Most terms of the separate escrow agreement relate to the mechanics of the parties' relationship with the escrow agent: storage of materials, payment of the agent,[3] etc. Those terms generally appear in a standard form contract from the escrow agent, and this book doesn't address them. This book does address terms governing the relationship between the recipient and provider. Those terms generally appear in the license agreement itself.

1. Deposit and Verification

The recipient should make sure the provider gives the escrow agent the right source code and supporting materials.

Escrow Deposit & Verification

(b) *Deposit.* Within two (2) Business Days of the Effective Date, Provider will deposit with the Escrow Agent, pursuant to the procedures of the Escrow Agreement, the source code for the Software, as well as all documentation necessary to enable a person of reasonable skill with software to compile and build machine-readable code for the Software, to maintain the Software, and to fully operate the Software. Promptly after release of any update, upgrade, patch, bug-fix, enhancement, new version, or other revision to the Software, Provider will deposit updated source code and documentation with the Escrow Agent. ("Deposit Material" refers to material required to be deposited pursuant to this Subsection 8(b).)

Currently, the largest U.S. escrow agent seems to be Iron Mountain (www.IronMountain.com).

3   Often it's the recipient who pays the escrow agent's fees, because the recipient benefits from making the source code available in this way. But the parties may split the fees, and there's no reason the provider can't pay.

> (c) *Verification.* At Recipient's request (and at Recipient's expense), the Escrow Agent may at any time verify the Deposit Material, including without limitation by compiling source code, running tests to compare it to the Software, and reviewing the completeness and accuracy of any and all material. In the event that the Escrow Agent informs Recipient that the Deposit Material does not conform to the requirements of Subsection 8(b) above: (i) Provider will promptly deposit conforming Deposit Material; and (ii) Provider will reimburse Recipient for subsequent verification of the new Deposit Material. Any breach of the provisions of Subsection 8(c)(i) above will constitute material breach of this Agreement, and no further payments will be due from Recipient until such breach is cured, in addition to such other remedies as Recipient may have.

The escrow clause should list the deposit material. It should also require that the material be sufficient for a reasonably educated technician to compile, run, and maintain the software, as in subsection (b) in the clause box above.

What if the provider deposits inadequate material? The recipient won't know what's been deposited unless and until it gets its hands on the material—after a release condition. By then, the provider will probably be out of business, or at least uncooperative, and it will be too late to insist on compliance. That's why many escrow clauses include verification procedures, as in subsection (c). The escrow agent checks to see if the provider deposited the right material. (This verification system is another reason to hire a professional escrow company, rather than use a trusty friend.)

2. License and Confidentiality

If the recipient does someday receive source code and other deposit material, it will need the right to exploit them. In other words, it will need a license.

> *Escrow License*
>
> (d) *License & Use.* Provider hereby grants Recipient a license to use, reproduce, and create derivative works from the Deposit Material. Recipient may not distribute or sublicense the Deposit Material or make any use of it whatsoever except for such internal use as is necessary to maintain and support the Software. The Deposit Material constitutes Confidential Information of Provider pursuant to Section 6 (Confidentiality). Nothing in this Subsection 8(d) will be construed to grant Recipient physical access to the Deposit Material except as provided in the Escrow Agreement.

In some cases, the contract's license clause already provides the necessary rights. If the software licensed—the "Licensed Product," or whatever—includes all elements of the code and documentation, including source code and other deposit material, no additional license is necessary. If not, the recipient will need a separate license, like the one in the clause box above. The license should include the same terms as the license to the underlying software, except that if the recipient is going to handle its own maintenance and support, it may also need the right to create derivative works.[4]

The license should be effective immediately, even though the recipient does not yet have access to the source code and may never get it. In other words, don't write: "Upon the occurrence of a Release Condition, Provider grants Recipient a license...." If the provider goes bankrupt, the law may rescind such a license, and the recipient won't have full rights to the material. The only license that can survive bankruptcy is one that's effective *before* bankruptcy proceedings start. That's why the example above provides: "Provider *hereby* grants Recipient a license...." That license is effective immediately.

Providers should make sure the license limits the recipient's rights to deposit material. After all, if the provider comes out of bankruptcy, or recovers from whatever kept it from supporting the software, it will still want to protect its source code. So the license should limit the recipient to internal use: it can only use the source code to support and maintain the software, as in the example above.

Providers should make sure the recipient protects the secrecy of the source code. If the contract has a confidentiality clause, the deposit material should be considered confidential information, as in the example above. If there is no confidentiality clause, the escrow clause should include confidentiality provisions.[5]

3. Release and Other Issues

What triggers release of material to the recipient? Any event can serve, but release conditions usually fall into two categories: (1) the provider has breached its obligation to support the software; and (2) the provider's going bankrupt or out of business. (In some deals, the release conditions appear in the escrow agreement, rather than the main contract.)

---

4   See *Standard End-User License*, Section I.A, on page 12, and *Software Licenses in General, Copyright License Rights*, Subsection I.C.1, on page 21.

5   See *Confidentiality/Nondisclosure*, Section II.H, on page 83.

Escrow Release Conditions

(e) *Release Conditions.* The term "Release Conditions," as used in the Escrow Agreement, refers to any of the following: (i) material breach by Provider of Section 3 (Maintenance & Support) of this Agreement, if such breach remains uncured thirty (30) or more days after Recipient's written notice; (ii) any failure of Provider to function as a going concern; (iii) appointment, application for, or consent to a receiver, trustee, or other custodian for Provider or its assets; (iv) Provider becomes insolvent or unable to pay its debts as they mature in the ordinary course or makes an assignment for the benefit of creditors; and (v) Provider is liquidated or dissolved, or any proceedings are commenced by or against Provider under any bankruptcy, insolvency, or debtor's relief law.

The provider should make sure the contract talks about "material" breaches of support obligations, not just any technical breach. It should also make sure a breach does not count as a release condition unless it goes uncorrected for some period of time, like thirty days. See the example in the clause box above.

What if, at some point, the recipient tells the escrow agent a release condition has occurred, and the provider disagrees? The escrow agent is caught in the middle. Usually, it's the escrow agreement that solves this problem, with an arbitration clause. In case of dispute, the escrow agent doesn't have to release the material until it gets an order from an arbitrator. That's a good solution, but it can cause problems for the recipient if the software is critical and urgently needs maintenance. So recipients should consider a contract clause calling for *expedited* arbitration: a very fast procedure available through many commercial arbitrators.[6]

Finally, the escrow agreement—rather than the license agreement—should usually include a termination clause. It should provide that, if the license agreement is terminated for any reason, other than breach by the provider, the escrow agent will return the escrow material to the provider.

---

6 Because escrow arbitration clauses usually appear in the escrow agreement, not in the underlying license contract, I haven't included one here. But see *Dispute Resolution*, Section II.Q, on page 107.

J. Software Audits

One of the advantages of software is that it's easily reproduced. That's also one of the problems with software. In a license or distribution agreement, the audit clause helps the provider protect against unauthorized copying and use.

The audit clause authorizes the provider to review the recipient's books and computers. The provider searches for copies in excess of the license, use beyond the scope authorized, or distribution without royalty payments.

> *Software Audit*
>
> Provider may audit Recipient's use of the Licensed Product on thirty (30) days' advanced written notice. Recipient will cooperate with the audit, including by providing access to any books, computers, records, or other information that relate or may relate to use of the Licensed Product. Such audit will not unreasonably interfere with Recipient's business activities. In the event that an audit reveals unauthorized use of the Licensed Product, Recipient will reimburse Provider for the reasonable cost of the audit, in addition to such other rights and remedies as Provider may have. Provider will not conduct an audit more than once per calendar year.

Audits can be a source of terror for recipients, because the law provides some high fees for copyright infringement.

K. Updates and Upgrades

Software licenses sometimes grant the recipient rights to new versions. The contract will generally state that these updates and upgrades become part of the licensed product—the "Software" or whatever—so the parties don't need to sign a new license agreement.

Updates & Upgrades

Provider will provide Recipient with copies of all new versions, updates, and upgrades of the Software (collectively, "Upgrades"), without additional charge, promptly after commercial release. Upon such release, Upgrades will become part of the "Software," subject (without limitation) to the license set forth in Section 2.

—

Provider will deliver all Minor Upgrades (as defined below) to Recipient promptly after release, and such Minor Upgrades will then become part of a the "Licensed Product." Recipient may acquire copies of Major Releases (as defined below) at a twenty percent (20%) discount off of Provider's standard retail price, and such Major Release will become part of the "Licensed Product." "Major Release" refers to any new version of the Licensed Product Provider releases commercially (at its sole discretion) with a new version number to the left of the version decimal point. "Minor Upgrade" refers to any other new version of the Licensed Product.

Often the provider wants to distinguish between minor upgrades and major new releases. If the recipient has rights to SuperSoft v. 3.00, it should get a free copy of 3.04, which corrects bugs and make minor improvements. But SuperSoft v. 4.00 has all-new features and may even cost more. So clauses like the second example in the box above require that the recipient pay for these "major releases," though sometimes at a discount.

L. Documentation

Proper use of software often requires documentation. These documents range from user manuals to design or architecture descriptions for programmers and system managers.[1] If documentation is necessary, a software license or assignment should require that the provider provide it.

Some software contracts define the "Licensed Product" to include both software and "all documentation customarily distributed with such software or reasonably necessary to operate it." With a definition like that, the license and delivery clauses will usually give the recipient all the necessary rights. But some contracts address documentation separately.

Documentation

Provider will provide such documentation as is reasonably necessary to operate the Software ("Documentation"). Provider will deliver the Documentation to Recipient with delivery of the Software and will revise the Documentation as reasonably necessary in the event of changes to the Software, without further charge. Recipient may reproduce any such Documentation as reasonably necessary to support internal use of the Software.

Documentation is written text, just like software, so recipients need a license to reproduce or otherwise exploit it. See the example in the clause box above.

Documentation requirements vary widely, so you will likely have to customize a clause to fit your deal.

---

1   Another type of documentation usually appears *within* source code, so it' not addressed here. This highly technical "code documentation" explains the software's intended operation. If the recipient gets source code, it should automatically get any embedded documentation.

M. Use of Trademarks

A trademark license is like a software copyright license. It authorizes use of trademarks without transferring ownership. Businesses use these licenses to facilitate marketing.

The contract generally doesn't need a trademark license if one party wants to issue a press release talking about its relationship with the other. But if a party wants to make extensive marketing use of the other party's name, it needs a trademark license (assuming the name is a trademark). Such "extensive" use would include putting the name on product packages, for instance, in a distribution relationship.[1] And use of logos almost always requires a license.

Use of Names and Trademarks

Recipient hereby grants Provider a license to include Recipient's primary logo, illustrated on Attachment B, in any customer list or press release announcing this Agreement, provided Provider first submits each such press release or customer list to Recipient and receives written approval, which approval will not unreasonably be withheld.

—

Provider hereby grants Distributor a license to reproduce its trademarks listed on Attachment A on marketing and advertising materials and packaging related to any Product (collectively, "Advertisements"); provided (i) the Product conforms to the quality requirements listed in Attachment B and (ii) Distributor observes Provider's standard guidelines on trademark usage, attached hereto as Attachment C, including any written amendment

---

[1] It's hard to define "extensive." If in doubt, get a license—or talk to an experienced attorney.

> provided by Recipient in its sole discretion. In the event that Provider noti-
> fies Distributor in writing that any Product or Advertisement (pending or
> published) does not conform to the requirements of the preceding sen-
> tence, Distributor will promptly withdraw it or remove all Provider trade-
> marks; provided that Provider will not unreasonably issue such notice.

The trademark owner should supervise use of its marks. It should review press releases, customer lists, and other marketing documents to make sure they're consistent with its public image. And in a distribution agreement, the trademark owner should check on the quality of any product sold using its trademarks. This type of supervision doesn't just make good business sense; it's necessary to preserve trademark rights. Trademarks are like friends: if you don't treat them well, you lose them. A *naked license*—a grant of trademark rights without supervision—can invalidate the trademark.

Both examples in the clause box above help avoid naked licensing by grant-ing supervision rights. In the first example, the trademark owner has to approve trademark usage in advance. That's the best system for the owner, but it's not always practical, particularly where the other party issues hundreds or thousands of ads. So the second example does away with advanced approval. Instead, it requires that the other party observe the owner's trademark usage guidelines. And if the owner does notice misuse of its mark, the other party has to withdraw the offending ad. The second example also addresses the quality of the underlying product—promising the owner that its trademark won't be associated with shoddy merchandise.

But contract language might not do the trick alone. To preserve trademark status, the owner should *actually supervise* use of its marks.

N. Training

Training clauses are most common in software licenses, though they may appear in any sale of software or systems. In these clauses, the provider promises to help the recipient learn how to operate a computer system.

> *Training*
>
> Provider will provide training courses on operation of the Licensed Product, at Recipient's Houston facility, at such times during business hours as Recipient may reasonably request. Each training course will last three (3) hours. Recipient may enroll up to twelve (12) of its staff-members in any training course, and Provider will provide a hard copy of the Licensed Product's standard training manual for each enrollee. Each training course will be taught by a technician with no fewer than three (3) years' full-time experience operating ConfuSoft software systems. Provider will provide the first ten (10) trainings without additional charge and will provide additional trainings at its standard rates.
>
> ---
>
> Without additional charge, Provider will provide such training on use of the Software as Recipient may reasonably request, and the parties will negotiate in good faith regarding the time and place of such training.

Some clauses provide significant detail about training parameters: duration and size of courses, expertise of instructors, cost (if any), etc.—as in the first example in the clause box above. But some training clauses leave the details out, on the assumption that the parties can work them out later.

Training is a professional service. So if training forms a major part of the transaction, review *Promise of Professional Services*, Section I.E, on page 39.

O. Non-Compete Clauses

A non-compete clause provides that one party won't compete with the other. These clauses are most common in professional services contracts, where the provider promises not to compete with the recipient. But a non-compete clause can appear in any contract. (Usually, it's the provider who promises not to compete, so this section covers provider non-competes. But in some cases, the recipient makes the promise.)

Recipients worry that providers will learn new techniques or make new contacts while providing services, then use them to compete with the recipient. Even if the provider accepts that logic, the parties will likely negotiate over the definition of "compete."

Many courts dislike non-compete clauses, and in some states (e.g., California), they're partly unenforceable.[1] Legal systems are particularly hostile to clauses that keep a party from making a decent living. These laws on non-compete clauses vary, so consider consulting a lawyer with experience on this issue for your state.

No Competition

During the term of this Agreement and for six (6) months after termination, Provider will not solicit or provide services to any customer or potential customer of Recipient identified to Provider in writing during the term of this Agreement, provided such writing is transmitted as a necessary step in facilitating the provision of services required by this Agreement. The provisions of the preceding sentence do not apply to customers or potential customers

---

1   Most contracts should include a severability clause, providing that one unenforceable term won't doom the whole contract. See *Severability*, Section III.K, on page 122.

Provider identified before the Effective Date, provided Provider can prove such earlier identification through documentary evidence.

—

During the term of this Agreement and for one (1) year following termination, Provider will not solicit or accept employment, including without limitation as an independent contractor, from any Customer (as defined in the next sentence). A "Customer" is: (a) any person or entity that purchased goods or services from Recipient during the term of this Agreement or during the six (6) months preceding the Effective Date; and (b) any person or entity Recipient identified as a potential purchaser of its goods or services in any electronic or hard copy document disclosed to Provider during the term of this Agreement. Provider will pay Recipient thirty percent (30%) of any payments received from any Customer for products or services provided in breach of this Section 11, as liquidated damages.

—

During the term of this Agreement and for two (2) years following termination, Provider will not accept employment from, work for, provide services to, set up, serve as a sole proprietor or partner or other stakeholder in, or operate any Competitor (as defined in the next sentence), or own more than one percent (1%) of the outstanding shares or securities representing the right to vote for the election of directors or other managing authority of any Competitor. A "Competitor" is any person or entity that sells or distributes footwear, retail or wholesale. In the event of breach of the provisions of this Section 11, Provider will pay Recipient the sum of $10,000 as liquidated damages.

Non-compete clauses generally restrict competition for some period—a month, a year, or several years. See all three examples in the clause box above.

A non-compete clause can address direct competition, indirect competition, or both. Direct competition involves selling to the recipient's customers or participating in a business that offers the same products or services. Recipients worry about direct competition when the provider works in the same field, or could. For instance, both parties could provide computer programming. All three examples in the clause box above address direct competition.

Indirect competition involves provision of services to competitors, not actual competition. The provider may provide computer system design, while the recipient sells shoes. But the recipient doesn't want the provider using knowledge of the recipient's systems to build systems for rival shoe-shops. The third example in the clause box addresses indirect competition.

The first example in the clause box above provides a narrow definition of competition—a definition favored by providers. The provider agrees not to use the recipient's customer lists to seek new clients. It can compete in other ways. And the customer lists in question must have been disclosed during the parties' collaboration. The clause doesn't prevent sales to customers the provider discovered through some other source, or to the recipient's listed customers, if the provider can prove it identified them before the contract. Finally, the recipient must have disclosed the customer lists for legitimate purposes— to facilitate provision of services. It can't just e-mail its entire list of customers, to restrict the provider.

The second two examples in the clause box provide broader definitions of competition. The recipient can't sell to any customer of the recipient or any potential customer identified during the term of the contract. And the recipient can't sell services to a competing business, or run such a business. Recipients generally favor these types of clauses. But the clause's real punch depends on the industry. The second clause forbids sales to customers who bought from the recipient during the six months before the contract. What if the recipient's customers buy every three years? The provider might not mind that clause so much, and the recipient might want to extend the pre-contract timeline to three years. The second clause also forbids sales to potential customers identified *in writing* during the project. What if the provider heard potential customers' names at staff meetings? Finally, the third clause forbids sale of services to competitors—to anyone in the recipient's business: shoe retail and wholesale, in this case. If the recipient also *manufactures* shoes, or advertises them, the provider might still be able to serve competitors.

In other words, the definition of competing activity depends on the nature of the recipient's business. This is a hard clause to write. Get creative where necessary. Maybe the recipient worries most about competitors nearby. The clause could forbid sales to competitors "in the State of Illinois" or "within 1,000 miles of Recipient's principal office." Or maybe the recipient only worries about *certain* competitors. The clause could forbid sales to "Menacing Force LLP, Leading Brand Solutions, Inc., and Nemesis Corporation."

Finally, most non-compete clauses provide for liquidated damages, as in the second two examples in the clause box. It will be difficult to determine the recipient's damages if the provider breaches the clause. So the liquidated damages provision fixes a damages amount. The amount may be a percent of the provider's revenues from a stolen customer, as in the second example, or a fixed fee, as in the third example. The key requirement is that the amount bear *some* relation to the recipient's likely losses. If you plan to include liquidated damages in a non-compete clause—usually a good idea for recipients—review Section II.P, on page 104.

P. Liquidated Damages

When one party breaches a contract, the other generally has a right to damages: to money that compensates for its injuries. But in some relationships, the parties know in advance that damages will be hard to estimate. So they specify the amount the breaching party will have to pay—in a liquidated damages clause.

Imagine the recipient wants customized software to improve efficiency, and the provider agrees to write it within four months. If the provider delivers late or not at all, the recipient will have wasted a lot of time. It will also have missed out on savings and business opportunities. But it's hard to put a dollar figure on lost time or improvements brought by an untried system. So instead of risking an expensive court battle over damages, the parties agree in advance on *liquidated* damages. The provider will pay $150 for every day of delay and $25,000 if it never delivers the software at all.

Courts will only enforce a liquidated damages clause if it meets two conditions. First, at the time the parties sign the contract, likely damages have to be uncertain or difficult to prove. Second, the damages have to be compensation for injuries, not a penalty. Penalty clauses are unenforceable. So the liquidated damages amount should roughly approximate the injured party's projected losses. Of course, you don't know how much the injured party would lose if the other party breached. But you can at least guess at a range and fix the liquidated damages somewhere in that range. It doesn't matter if you guess wrong. What matters is that, at the point of executing the contract, the guess was reasonable. If the parties just pick some high number, with little or no relationship to likely losses, a court will probably consider it a penalty.

A liquidated damages clause should have two parts: a specification of damages and a justification.

Specification of Liquidated Damages

Provider will credit Recipient one percent (1%) of the License Fee, not to exceed twenty percent (20%), as liquidated damages, for each Business Day between the Due Date and any later date Provider actually delivers the Software.

———

In the event that Recipient materially breaches this Agreement and Provider terminates on that basis, Recipient will pay Provider, as liquidated damages, one third (1/3) of the Service Fees not yet invoiced.

———

In the event that the System does not provide the functionality listed in Items 1 through 5 of the Technical Specifications, Provider will pay Recipient $40,000.00, as liquidated damages.

The parties can set a specific dollar amount as liquidated damages, as in the last example in the clause box above. Or they can provide a formula to calculate damages, as in the first two examples.

Liquidated damages are generally exclusive: the injured party can't get any compensation except those damages. But some contracts provide that liquidated damages are not exclusive. For instance: "these liquidated damages do not preclude the injured party from seeking additional damages." In most states, a provision like that would not be enforceable.

The justification part of the clause addresses the requirements for liquidated damages. The parties agree that the liquidated damages are necessary because figuring actual losses would be so hard. They also agree that they didn't intend the clause as a penalty and that they used an estimate of actual losses to set the liquidated damages amount.

Justification for Liquidated Damages

The parties agree that the damages set forth in this Section are liquidated damages and not penalties and that they are reasonable in light of the harm that will be caused by breach, the difficulties of proof of loss, and the inconvenience and infeasibility of otherwise obtaining an adequate remedy.

The fact that the parties state these justification claims doesn't make them so. A court will make its own assessment. But neither party should be able to argue that it didn't understand the clause's purpose.

Q. Dispute Resolution

Dispute resolution clauses aim to keep the parties out of court. They provide alternate procedures for resolving arguments.

Dispute Resolution

In the event of dispute, either party may call for escalation through written notice to the other. Within three (3) Business Days of such notice, each party will designate an executive with authority to make commitments that would resolve the dispute ("Senior Manager"). The parties' Senior Managers will meet in person or by telephone ("Dispute Conference") within five Business Days of their designation and will negotiate in good faith to resolve the dispute. Except to the extent necessary to prevent irreparable harm or to preserve rights or remedies, neither party will initiate arbitration or litigation until thirty (30) business days after the Dispute Conference.

—

Any claim arising out of or related to this Agreement will be submitted to mandatory, binding arbitration under the auspices of Geriatric Judges, Inc., in St. Paul, Minnesota, with the parties sharing equally the costs of arbitration. The preceding sentence does not limit either party's right to provisional or ancillary remedies from a court of competent jurisdiction before, after, or during the pendency of any arbitration, and the exercise of any such remedy does not waive either party's right to arbitration.

Escalation is the least formal dispute resolution procedure. It calls on the parties to bump the argument up to senior executives, as in the first example in the clause box above. An escalation clause should provide that no one can file a lawsuit until the senior executives have met and tried to resolve the dispute.

Arbitration is more common. In clauses like the second example above, the parties agree to let a third party decide their dispute. The clause can name the arbitrator in advance, or it can authorize the parties to pick one or more arbitrators. Three-person panels are common: "Each party will select an arbitrator, who has no financial or family relationship with such party, and identify him or her in writing within ten days. The two arbitrators will select a third arbitrator within fifteen days." IT companies, however, often turn the matter over to a well-known arbitration company, like AAA or JAMS.[1] Those companies generally provide procedures for choosing the arbitrator or arbitrators, as well as for running the arbitration. They usually hire lawyers and retired judges to serve as arbitrators.

If arbitration is "mandatory," either party can force it on the other. In other words, even if one party wants to sue in court, the other can switch the case to arbitration.[2] Arbitration generally should be mandatory because, if not, someone will likely refuse. Arbitration should also be "binding." Otherwise, it risks wasting everyone's time. In binding arbitration, the arbitrator's decision is final. The losing party can't get the decision reversed by a court, even if the arbitrator misunderstood the law or facts. In most jurisdictions, binding arbitration can be overturned only if the arbitrator abused his or her discretion through clearly improper behavior, which is rare.

Some disputes require quick resolution, so the clause may call for *expedited* arbitration. For instance: "The parties will submit briefs within three (3) business days of selection of the arbitrator; the arbitrator will hold a hearing within three (3) business days of submission of briefs; and the arbitrator will issue the decision within five (5) business days of the hearing." Also, arbitration companies often provide procedures for expedited arbitration. So the clause might read: "In the event that the arbitration relates to release of source code for the Mission Critical Application, arbitration will proceed pursuant to

1   AAA is the American Arbitration Association (www.adr.org). JAMS originally stood for "Judicial Arbitration and Mediation Service," but now the company's name is just "JAMS" (www.jamsadr.com).
2   Courts sometimes won't force arbitration on an unwilling plaintiff, despite "mandatory" language in the contract. Some state courts, for instance, won't enforce an arbitration clause in a shrinkwrap contract, out of concern the plaintiff didn't realize he or she was giving up the right to a court.

Geriatric Judges, Inc.'s *Rules for Expedited Decision,* and the parties will take all required actions as promptly as reasonably possible."

Mediation is another dispute resolution procedure, though it rarely appears in software and services contracts. In a mediation clause, the parties agree to work with a third party who can help resolve the dispute. The mediator often tries to broker a deal, including by helping each party see the pros and cons of litigating. The mediator has no authority to decide the case. A mediation clause might read: "In the event of dispute, the parties will participate in at least four hours of mediation under the auspices of Henry Clay Mediation Services, LLC. The parties will share equally all costs related to mediation."

R. Term and Termination

Termination clauses address four issues. First, when, if ever, will the contract terminate naturally? What is its *term* or duration? Second, when can a party terminate for cause? Third, when, if ever, can a party terminate for convenience (for any reason or no reason)? Fourth, what happens after termination?

Some contracts don't need term and termination provisions. In a simple purchase agreement, for example, termination would not make sense. The provider provides the goods, and then the deal is done. There's nothing to terminate. Term and termination clauses make the most sense in contracts with continuing rights or obligations—like most software licenses and services contracts.

1. Term

The term is the period during which the contract operates: its duration. The word implies something temporary, like a senator's "term" of office.

Term

This Agreement will continue until terminated by either party as specifically authorized herein.

—

This Agreement will terminate on Recipient's acceptance of the Final Deliverable (as defined in Section 3).

—

> This Agreement will remain in effect for one (1) year from the date of execution by both parties. Thereafter, it will renew for successive one (1) year periods, unless either party refuses such renewal by written notice thirty (30) or more days before the end of the current term.

In some contracts, the parties' rights and obligations continue indefinitely. In that case, use an open-ended term, continuing until someone terminates, as in the first example in the clause box above. The parties can also select a more definite end-date—one year from signing, for instance—as in the last two examples in the clause box.

Term clauses often authorize one or both parties to extend the term. If the term can be extended indefinitely, it should require both parties' consent, so no one is forced into a never-ending deal. See the last example in the clause box.[1]

2. Termination for Cause

Termination for cause happens when something has gone wrong.

> *Termination for Cause*
>
> Either party may terminate this agreement for material breach by written notice, effective in thirty (30) days, unless the other party first cures such breach.
>
> —
>
> Either party may terminate this Agreement for cause by written notice, without opportunity to cure, in the event that: (a) the other party fails to function as a going concern; (b) a receiver, trustee, or other custodian for the other party or its assets is appointed, applied for, or consented to; (c) the other party becomes insolvent or unable to pay its debts as they mature in the ordinary course; (d) the other party makes an assignment for the benefit of creditors; or (e) the other party is liquidated or dissolved, or any proceedings are commenced by or against it under any bankruptcy, insolvency, or debtor's relief law.

---

[1] The last example in the clause box is an automatic renewal or "evergreen" clause. Some states won't enforce these clauses against consumers, in some circumstances. In those cases, contract is usually considered month-to-month after the first term.

The usual *cause* for termination is breach of contract. Some clauses clarify that the breach must be "material," as in the first example in the clause box. That means a minor breach, like paying a day late, will not authorize termination. The law generally reaches the same conclusion, but there's no harm in clarity.

Often, termination for breach clauses requires advanced notice—thirty days is common—and an opportunity to cure, as in the first example. If the breaching party fixes the breach, the contract is not terminated. But a cure period isn't required. Advanced notice isn't required either, though the clause should at least require written notice.

Sometimes the parties need the right to terminate for cause even without a breach. Either party might want to escape if the other goes bankrupt, as in the second example in the clause box. (Bankruptcy will probably threaten payment, provision of services, or other ongoing obligations.) Other causes allowing termination for cause could include the departure of a key employee or the end of a relationship with an important third party. Often, these other *causes* don't require advanced notice or an opportunity to cure.

3. Termination for Convenience

Termination for convenience is an escape hatch. It lets a party get out for any reason or for no reason at all. If you're afraid the contract might become burdensome because of some business change you can't predict, consider a termination for convenience clause.

Termination For Convenience

Either party may terminate this Agreement for convenience on sixty (60) days' advanced written notice.

—

Recipient may terminate this Agreement for convenience upon ninety (90) days' advanced written notice. On the date of such termination, Recipient will pay Provider a termination fee of thirty percent (30%) of the fees for Services not yet provided.

Termination for convenience often requires more notice than the traditional thirty days, as in both examples in the clause box above.

Many contracts impose a price on termination for convenience. The party terminating has to pay a fee. The fee should represent a rough guess at the other party's losses caused by termination. For instance, in a services contract, the provider might spend time and money hiring or reassigning staff to serve the recipient's needs. If the recipient terminates early, the provider should get fees that more or less match that cost. Or in a software license, recipient might rely on the software, only to have it taken away when the provider terminates for convenience. The fee would compensate the recipient for the dislocation caused by the loss of the software.

4. Effects of Termination

Termination doesn't mean the contract disappears—that it becomes null and void. In fact, some clauses can continue in force. Rather, termination ends the flow of goods and services. In a software license, the recipient loses its license rights (usually). In a services contract, the provider no longer has to provide the services.

> *Effects of Termination*
>
> Upon termination of this Agreement, Recipient will cease all use of the Software, and each party will promptly return any property of the other's. The following provisions will survive termination of this Agreement: any obligation of Recipient to pay for Software used or services rendered before termination; Sections 7 (Indemnity), 8 (Limitation of Liability), 9(b) (Nondisclosure of Confidential Information), 11 (Arbitration), 12 (Notices), and 14 (Miscellaneous); and any other provision of this Agreement that must survive termination to fulfill its essential purpose.

The contract clauses that survive termination fall into three categories: (1) rights and obligations triggered by termination, (2) continuing rights and obligations, and (3) clauses governing the relationship.

First, the contract should list rights or obligations triggered by termination—if any. For instance, in most license agreements, the recipient should promise to stop using the software after termination.[1] And in many contracts,

---

1 Many providers leave this provision out because they assume termination of the contract will also terminate the recipient's right to use the software. But as Section I.C explains, it's not clear anyone needs a license to *use* software. If the recipient always had the right to use software in its possession, the contract's termination won't end that right. That's why, if the provider wants to be sure the recipient's usage rights will end, the contract should specifically state that the recipient won't use the software after termination. See *Software Licenses in General, Copyright License Rights*, Use (a pseudo-right), in Subsection 1.C.1, on page 24.

each party should promise to return the other's property. Some of these "triggered provisions" will already appear in other clauses, like confidentiality and technology escrow. If not, the termination clause itself should list them, as in the example in the clause box above.

Second, if any rights or obligations will continue after termination, the contract should list them and state that they continue or "survive termination," as in the example above. For instance, what if the confidentiality clause requires nondisclosure for three years? That obligation should not end just because the contract terminates after nine months. The termination clause should provide that the parties' nondisclosure obligations survive termination. To take another example, some software licenses are perpetual and irrevocable. In those cases, the termination clause should list the license as one of the sections that survive termination.[2]

Third, termination has no impact on clauses governing the contractual relationship. These "governing clauses" include provisions about dispute resolution, assignment of contracts, notices, limitations of liability, definitions, and severability.[3] The termination clause doesn't have to state that these provisions survive because it's usually obvious. But why take chances? The example in the clause box lists these governing clauses. And just to be sure nothing has been left out, many termination clauses preserve "any provision that must survive to fulfill its essential purpose." Again, see the example in the clause box.

---

2   See *Software Licenses in General, Scope Terms*, Subsection I.C.2, on page 25. A perpetual license should survive the term of the contract, but it ends if someone terminates. An irrevocable license should survive any termination, but it ends when the term ends. And a license that is both perpetual and irrevocable should survive the term and any termination. Make sure your termination clause reflects that structure.

3   See *Dispute Resolution*, Section II.Q, on page 107; *Assignment*, Section III.I, on page 121; *Notices*, Section III. F, on page 119; *Limitation of Liability*, Section II.G, on page 78; *Definitions*, Section III.B, on page 117; and *Severability*, Section III.K, on page 122.

S. Everything Else

What have the parties negotiated? Whatever the terms are, write them in clear, simple English. As the Introduction explains, good contracts are customized. Contract-drafting is a creative process, like doing business itself, so don't hesitate to blaze new trails. Just think through what you're trying to say, then write it down.

III. Supporting Clauses

The supporting clauses include terms many professionals call "boilerplate," as well as introductory material like recitals and definitions. These clauses are usually less sensitive than the general clauses and transactional clauses, and they generate less debate. But that doesn't necessarily make them less important. You can't tell what issue will crop up in a contractual relationship, so you never know when one of these supporting clauses will become vital.

The descriptions below don't included clause boxes. Most, however, start with a section- and page-number reference to the full-length contract in the Appendix on page 125. Look there for examples of these clauses.

A. Introduction and Recitals

See Appendix, 1st five paragraphs, page 126.
A contract's introduction generally identifies the parties and the contract itself. The recitals explain why the parties are doing business and sometimes give a little of their history. Neither introduction nor recitals is absolutely necessary. The contract's first line could read: "BluntCo, LLC hereby agrees to provide the following services to Laconic Industries, Inc. ...." But recitals are usually a good idea because they make the contract easier to understand.

The introduction and recitals should include no operative clauses: no promises, no rights, and no obligations. They might define a few terms, but otherwise they're just introductory.

However, the last recital does traditionally include some valuable language. It states that the contract has "consideration" or "adequate consideration," as in the last recital in the Appendix. Consideration means something is exchanged: the document doesn't record a one-way transaction, like a gift. A court won't enforce an agreement without consideration. A recital's claim of consideration doesn't guarantee a court will agree, but it can help[1]

B. Definitions

See Appendix Section 1, page 126.
As the introduction explains, most contracts create various terms, define them, and then use them repeatedly.[2] These definitions can be scattered throughout the contract. That's fine for terms used in only one clause. But if Section 4 defines a term, and other sections use it, readers might have trouble finding the

---

1   Consideration lies outside the scope of this book. If you're concerned that your deal lacks consideration—lacks a two-way exchange—consult an experienced IT contracts attorney.

2   See *The Structure of a Contract and of this Book*, on page 5.

term's definition. So it's usually a good idea to collect all the defined terms used in more than one section and put them in a single definitions clause. That clause is usually Section 1—and it lists the defined terms in alphabetical order. As with all contract terms, definitions should be as simple and clear as possible.

C. Time Is of the Essence

If a contract says "time is of the essence," even the slightest delay by either party is a material breach, at least in theory. In reality, almost no one intends such a harsh rule, so the clause's meaning requires guesswork. Which of the parties' deadlines absolutely must be met, and which don't? Because the clause is so vague, you should generally leave it out. If time is critical for some action, the contract should say so: "Any failure of Provider to deliver the Mission Critical Module on or before its due-date constitutes a material breach of this Agreement." (The example in the Appendix does not include a time clause.)

D. Independent Contractors

See Appendix Subsection 14(a), page 134.
An independent contractor clause confirms that the parties are not partners, in the legal sense. They also aren't principal and agent or employer and employee. They're separate. The point is to avoid the tax implications and other legal consequences that can flow from "dependent" relationships, and to make sure neither party can make legal commitments on the other's behalf.

E. Choice of Law and Jurisdiction

See Appendix Subsection 14(f), page 135.
A choice of law clause picks the state whose laws will govern the contract. The clause usually also picks the courts with jurisdiction over disputes. The latter choice is often more important because laws are similar, but fighting a case downtown is a lot easier than fighting a thousand miles away. Each party should try for the courts closest to home, or closest to its lawyers. Ideally, you will pick the same state's law, because that's easier to manage. But it's actually possible to pick New York law and Alabama courts.[3]

---

3   If you have an arbitration clause or some other dispute resolution procedure, the choice of law clause tells the arbitrator what law to apply. And the jurisdiction part of the clause determines what court should enforce the arbitrator's decision.

If you don't make a choice in the contract, courts will choose for you—usually selecting the law and court with the closest connection to the contract. If the parties are in different states (or countries), it's often hard to say which a court will choose. So a choice of law clause reduces uncertainty.

Some choice of law clauses disqualify two particular laws: the 1980 United Nations Convention on Contracts for the International Sale of Goods (the "UN Convention") and the Uniform Computer Information Transactions Act ("UCITA"). The UN Convention governs some contracts between parties in different nations. Clauses like the example in the Appendix exclude it because the parties want Wyoming law or Texas law or whatever, and they don't want to think about whether the UN Convention applies. UCITA, on the other hand, is a purely American affair. It's a proposed law that has a lot of people up in arms. Recipients in particular say UCITA unfairly limits their rights and remedies. Few states have adopted UCITA, but many recipients and providers exclude it, just in case their state ever does adopt it: "This Agreement will not be governed by the Uniform Computer Information Transactions Act as adopted in any jurisdiction." (The example in the Appendix does not exclude UCITA.)

F. Notices

See Appendix Section 12, page 133.
A notices provision provides an address for each party to receive official notices. The idea is that, if someone wants to terminate or take some other action requiring notice, it has a legally effective address. If the notice-recipient moves without telling the sender, and some notice doesn't get through, the termination or whatever is still effective. The failure to communicate is the notice-recipient's own fault.

Many notice provisions, like the example in the Appendix, provide a mechanism for notices. Notices will be considered received, whether they actually were or not, if sent by certified mail or whatever other mechanism the notice clause chooses.

G. Government Restricted Rights

Federal regulations give the U.S. government some surprising rights to software. If a federal agency has software developed, or receives it under certain other circumstances, it gets "unlimited license rights." The agency can make as many copies as it wants, share the software with other federal agencies and with the public, etc. Obviously, this could cost the provider a lot of sales. So providers of commercial software, or of any software not created for the feds, often include a clause addressing federal rights. The clause clarifies that the software *is not* subject to unlimited rights. Rather, it's commercial software, licensed with "restricted rights."

Government restricted rights clauses sometimes appear in standard contract forms—forms used for both government and non-government deals. So even if you're not working on a federal contract, you may run into a clause like the one at the end of this section. If you're the recipient and you don't plan to share the software with the feds, the clause shouldn't restrict you in any important way. (Many clauses do require that you leave various notices on the software and its packaging.) And if you're the provider and you see *no* chance of distribution to the federal government, you don't need the clause. Some providers, however, include it just in case.

If you're a provider and you are licensing to the federal government, or to distributors who might do so, add a government restricted rights clause. But first consider consulting an attorney who specializes in government contracting and who also knows IT. Dealing with the federal government presents a lot of legal pitfalls. (A government contracts attorney can also help you place proper government restricted rights notices in your software and on its packaging—and can help with state government contracts too.)

The example contract in the Appendix doesn't include a government restricted rights clause. The following, however, is sample language: "The Software is provided with Restricted Rights. Use, duplication, or disclosure for or by the government of the United States, including without limitation any of its agencies or instrumentalities, is subject to restrictions set forth, as applicable: (i) in subparagraphs (a) through (d) of the *Commercial Computer Software—Restricted Rights* clause at FAR 52.227-19; (ii) in subparagraph (c)(1)(ii) of the *Rights in Technical Data and Computer Software* clause at DFARS 252.227-7013; or (iii) in similar clauses in other federal regulations, including the NASA FAR supplement. The contractor or manufacturer is Protecto Systems, Inc. Recipient will not remove or deface any restricted rights notice or other legal notice appearing in the Software or on any packaging or other media associated with the Software. Recipient will require that its customers, distributors, and other recipients of the Software agree to and acknowledge the provisions of this Section 13, in writing."[4]

---

4   "FAR" refers to the Federal Acquisition Regulations. "DFARS" refers to the Defense Federal Acquisition Regulations. And some clauses use a third set of initials, "CFR," for the Code of Federal Regulations.

H. Technology Export

See Appendix Subsection 14(d), page 134.

U.S. law restricts the export of certain technologies, particularly encryption software, which has military and intelligence uses. To avoid liability to the government, software providers often have customers promise to obey those laws. The example in the appendix is a simple clause, where the recipient promises to obey all U.S. export laws and regulations. If the recipient has distributors or sublicensees, the clause should go further: "Recipient will require that all its distributors, sublicensees, customers, and other recipients of the Software sign a written agreement promising to comply with all applicable U.S. laws and regulations related to export of the Software." Some providers go even further and require an indemnification from the recipient. If the recipient breaches the export laws, it will defend the provider against any government or other lawsuit, and pay any fees or other damages.[5]

Of course, foreign laws also address technology export. If the provider is concerned about a particular country, it should have an attorney licensed there prepare the clause. An international "catch-all" clause may also provide some protection: "Recipient will not export or transmit the Software across any national boundary except in compliance with all applicable laws and regulations, including without limitation the export laws and regulations of the originating country."

Providers of sensitive technology, however, shouldn't rely on contract clauses for protection. They should become familiar with export laws and seek legal advice on steps to prevent illegal export.

I. Assignment

See Appendix Subsection 14(e), page 134.

An assignment clause states whether a party may transfer the contract—with all its rights and obligations—to someone else. The clause can forbid all assignments, or let only one party assign the contract, or permit any assignment. Many clauses, like the example in the Appendix, permit assignment only in case of a merger or acquisition.[6]

---

5   See *Indemnity*, Section II.F, on page 75.

6   This section refers to assignments of an entire contract, not of intellectual property. For those assignments, see *Software Ownership: Assignment and Work-for-Hire, Assignments*, Section I.D.1, on page 33.

J. Force Majeure

See Appendix Subsection 14(c), page 134.
A force majeure clause says the parties are not responsible for their contractual obligations if acts of God or other forces out of their control interfere. A court might reach the same conclusion, but the clause removes doubt.

K. Severability

See Appendix Subsection 14(g), page 135.
A severability clause limits the impact of an unenforceable clause. It confirms that the parties intend the contract to operate as written to the maximum extent possible. They don't want the deal to fall apart, or partially fall apart, if one or more clauses can't be enforced. For instance, non-compete clauses sometimes aren't fully enforceable.[7] A severability clause confirms that the parties still intend the recipient to have the maximum protection possible against competition.

Clauses like the example in the Appendix also try to preserve the contract, as written, by having each party waive any legal rights that would prevent full enforcement. The waiver itself might not be enforceable, but it's worth a shot.

L. No Waiver

See Appendix Subsection 14(b), page 134.
Big companies sometimes fail to notice when someone has breached one of their contracts. So they often include a no-waiver clause. This clause provides that a party's failure to sue quickly will not waive its right to do so—and that failure to respond to one breach doesn't waive the right to respond to another.

M. Conflicts among Attachments

See Appendix Subsection 14(h), page 135.
Many contracts include one or two attachments, and contracts for complex deals can include ten or more. (*Attachment A: Technical Specifications; Attachment B: Schedule for Services; Attachment C: NDA; Attachment D....*) What happens if the terms of these attachments contradict each other or contradict the contract's main body? What if the main body says the provider is supposed to assign four technicians, and Attachment B says three?

---

7   See *Non-Compete Clauses*, Section II.O, on page 100.

You'd think a little care would eliminate this risk. But you can't predict every possible interpretation of the contract. Plus, some attachments could be forms attached to the contract without a lot of thought. And others, like Statements of Work, may be drafted in the future—possibly by someone who didn't read the contract. So a conflicts clause can prevent a lot of confusion.

Most clauses simply provide that, in the event of conflict, the main body overrides the attachments, as in the example in the Appendix. That doesn't address the issue of conflicts among the other attachments, so some go further and create a complete order of precedence. For instance: "In the event of any conflict among the various exhibits to this Agreement and this main body, the following order of precedence will govern, with lower numbers overruling higher ones: (1) this main body of this Contract; (2) any Statement of Work, with more recent Statements of Work taking precedence over later ones; (3) Exhibit A; (4) Exhibit B; (5) Exhibit C."

Don't let the conflicts clause become an excuse for sloppy drafting. You should still review every attachment and eliminate conflicting terms.

N. Construction

Courts generally construe vague terms against the party that wrote them. In other words, if one party wrote the contract (e.g., a clickwrap), a court will construe or interpret vague terms in a way that favors the *other* party. Construction clauses seek to eliminate that rule. The parties agree that there will be no favoritism in construction: "The parties agree that the terms of this Agreement result from negotiations between them. This Agreement will not be construed in favor of or against either party by reason of authorship." (The example in the Appendix does not include a construction clause.)

O. Entire Agreement

See Appendix Section 14(i), page 135.

The entire agreement or "integration" clause confirms that all terms the parties meant to include are *in* the agreement. It voids any letters, discussions, side-agreements, or anything of that kind existing before the contract was signed. Clauses like the example in the Appendix go even further and provide that the contract can't be amended except through a written document signed by both parties.

Appendix: Contract Form

This appendix provides a full-length contract form—and you can download an electronic copy at this book's website: www.TechContracts.net. The form represents a combination contract: a sale of both software and services. It's included because combination contracts include the key terms for both types of deals. If you want to use the form to help write or understand a contract that is not a combination, just delete or ignore the terms that don't fit. For instance, if your contract is a software license that doesn't involve services, delete the services clause (Section 2).

You are very welcome to use this form for your own agreements. But if you do, consider it no more than a starting point—and not just because your deal may not call for a combination contract. A generic form will *always* need adjustment to fit a deal. Review it carefully, compare it with the terms of your planned deal, and if possible, get a lawyer's help.

The form below tries to strike a balance between providers' and recipients' needs. You might be better off starting with a more *slanted* form. And if you do use this form, consider revising it to *create* more slant. Form contracts used by software and services vendors generally favor the provider. They have narrow warranties, broad limitations of liability, strict payment terms, etc. Forms used by IT recipients often favor the recipient—with broad warranty clauses, strict delivery deadlines, etc.

Where else can you find sample contracts? They're available online and through commercial forms books. And of course, you can get a form from a lawyer. Even if you don't have an in-house attorney or other easy access to legal help, you shouldn't have to spend a fortune to get a form. Lawyers usually have lots of forms, and a good IT attorney probably won't need a lot of time to find one similar to your deal. If a lawyer is willing to give you a form, you can do the work of fitting it to your deal and save money. Of course, the lawyer will send you a note saying, essentially: "I'm just giving you this form, not any legal advice. If you screw up your deal, it's not my fault, and I'm not liable." Don't be offended. He or she has to do that. (And the lawyer is making a good point. There's no substitute for a good attorney, and if you can afford it, you *should* have him or her revise the form to fit the deal, instead of doing it yourself.) In fact, as this book's introduction explains, the form below and this entire book come with the same precaution—all the more so because I'm not your lawyer.

If your company signs a lot of software and services contracts, consider making your own standard form. Ideally, you would have a standard contract that doesn't need much revision for each new deal. It should be drafted to suit your particular needs, and usually it should be slanted to favor your interests. (You can always reduce the slant during negotiations if the other party objects.) If possible, have a lawyer prepare the company's standard form. It's one thing to risk non-expert drafting on a single deal, but this form will lie at the heart of every contract you execute. For the price of one contract, you can apply legal expertise to all your deals.

Sample Contract

TECHNOLOGY LICENSE & INTEGRATION SERVICES AGREEMENT

This Technology License & Services Agreement (this "Agreement") is entered into as of _____, 20__ (the "Effective Date") by and between _____, a _____ ("Recipient"), and _____, a _____ ("Provider").

WHEREAS Provider provides software applications that _____; and

WHEREAS Recipient and Provider have agreed that Provider will develop and license to Recipient a software application for the purpose of _____; and

WHEREAS Recipient and Provider have also agreed that Provider will provide Recipient with maintenance and support services related to such software;

NOW, THEREFORE, in consideration of the mutual covenants, terms, and conditions set forth below, including those outlined on Attachments A and B (which are incorporated into this Agreement by this reference), the adequacy of which consideration is hereby accepted and acknowledged, the parties agree as follows:

1. Definitions

(a) "Documentation" refers to: (i) a manual for end-users that explains the functionality of the Software in language simple enough for a non-technician to understand, in Provider's reasonable opinion; (ii) updates of such end-user manual created pursuant to Provider's obligations set forth in Section 2(b) below; and (iii) such other Software documentation as the parties may mutually agree.

(b) "Facility" refers to Recipient's facility located at _____.

(c) "Software" refers to the software application to be created pursuant to this Agreement, described in Attachment A, as well as any revision created pursuant to Provider's obligations set forth in Section 2(b) below.

(d) "Technical Specifications" refers to the Software technical specifications attached to this Agreement as Attachment A.

(e) "Warranty Period" refers to the ____-day period following Acceptance (as defined in Section 4).

2. Services

(a) *Customization & Integration.* Provider will: (i) design and develop the Software so that it performs materially in accordance with its Technical Specifications; and (ii) write the Documentation. Provider will provide the services required in this Subsection 2(a) on the schedule set forth in Part I of Attachment B.

(b) *Maintenance & Support.* Starting on Acceptance of the Software pursuant to Section 4 below, Provider will maintain and support the Software so that it performs materially in accordance with its Technical Specifications. Provider's maintenance and support obligations include, without limitation, the tasks listed in Part II of Attachment B. Provider will provide such maintenance and support services through no fewer than _____ technicians with the following qualifications: _____.

3. License

(a) *Grant of Rights.* Effective upon receipt of the Final Milestone payment listed in Section 5(a) below, Provider grants Recipient a fully paid, perpetual, non-exclusive license to reproduce and use ____ copies of the Software's object code and as many copies of the Documentation as are reasonably required to support use of such copies of the Software. The rights granted in this Section 3(a) are not extended to any parent, subsidiary, or affiliate of Recipient.

(b) *Restrictions.* Provider retains full title to and ownership of the Software and Documentation, and Recipient receives no rights to the Software other than those specifically granted in this Section 3. Without limiting the generality of the foregoing,[1] Recipient will not: (i) modify, create derivative works from, distribute, or sublicense the Software; (ii) use the Software for service bureau or time-sharing purposes or in any other way that allows third parties to use or benefit directly from the Software; or (iii) reverse engineer, decompile, disassemble, or otherwise attempt to derive any of the Software's source code.

4. Delivery & Acceptance

Provider will install the Software at, and deliver the Documentation to, the Facility on or before _____ ("Delivery"). Upon Delivery, Recipient may perform such tests as it sees fit to determine whether the Software conforms to its Technical Specifications. The Software will be considered accepted: (a) when Recipient provides Provider written notice of acceptance, or (b) thirty (30) days after Delivery, if Recipient has not first provided Provider with written notice of rejection (collectively, "Acceptance"). Recipient may reject the Software only in the event that it materially deviates from its Technical Specifications. In the event of such rejection, Provider will, at its option, (i) repair the Software and re-deliver and re-install it within fifteen (15) days, or (ii) refund all amounts paid pursuant to this Agreement. Re-delivery and re-installation pursuant to the previous sentence will be considered another Delivery, and the parties will again follow the acceptance procedures set forth in this Section 4, except that in the event of rejection, Recipient may elect to terminate this Agreement and receive a full refund of all amounts paid pursuant to this Agreement. The refunds authorized by this Section 4 are not exclusive of any other remedies Recipient may have. Upon any termination and refund pursuant to this Section, Recipient will return all copies of the Software and Documentation.

5. Payment

(a) *Development Services & License.* Recipient will pay Provider the following amounts, each subject to invoice upon the milestones listed in Part I of Attachment B:

---

1   For an explanation of this phrase, see the footnote on page 14.

- Milestone 1: $_____.
- Milestone 2: $_____.
- Final Milestone: $_____.

(b) *Maintenance & Support Services.* For services listed in Section 2(b) above, Recipient will pay Provider $_____ per calendar month, in advance, starting after expiration of the Warranty Period.

(c) *Invoices.* Provider will submit itemized invoices to Recipient for the payments required in this Section 5, and all invoices will be due and payable within thirty (30) days.

6. Warranties

(a) *Function.* Provider warrants that, during the Warranty Period, the Software will perform materially as described in the Technical Specifications. However, Provider provides no warranty regarding, and will have no responsibility for any claim arising out of: (i) a modification made by Recipient, unless Provider approves such modification in writing; or (ii) use of the Product in combination with or on products other than as specified in the Technical Specifications or authorized in writing by Provider. In the event of breach of the warranty set forth in this Subsection 6(a), in addition to Provider's obligations set forth in Section 2(b) above, Provider will: (A) promptly repair or replace the Software, or if such attempts do not succeed after sixty (60) days, (B) refund all amounts paid by Recipient pursuant to this Agreement. In the event of option (B) above, Recipient will return all copies of the Software and Documentation. The remedies set forth in this Section 6(a) are not exclusive of any others Recipient may have.

(b) *Infringement/Ownership.* Provider warrants that it is and will be the owner of the Software and of each and every component thereof, including without limitation of intellectual property rights, or the recipient of a valid license thereto, and that it has and will maintain the full power and authority to grant the rights in the Software granted in this Agreement without the further consent of any person or entity. If the Software becomes, or in either party's reasonable opinion is likely to become, the subject of any claim, suit, or proceeding arising from or alleging infringement of any intellectual property right, or in the event of any adjudication that the Software infringes on any such right, Provider, at its own expense, will promptly take the following actions: (i) secure for Recipient the right to continue using the Software, or if that effort fails; (ii) replace or modify the Software to make it noninfringing, provided that such modification or replacement will not materially degrade the operation or performance of the Software. The remedies set forth in this Section 6(b) are not exclusive of any others Recipient may have.

(c) *Harmful Code.* Provider warrants that the Software and any media used to distribute it contain no viruses or other computer instructions or technological means whose purpose is to disrupt, damage, or interfere with the use of computers or related systems.

(d) *Right to Do Business.* Each party warrants that it has the full right and authority to enter into, execute, and perform its obligations under this Agreement and that no pending or threatened claim or litigation known to such party would have a material adverse impact on its ability to perform as required by this Agreement.

(e) *Exclusions.* EXCEPT FOR THE EXPRESS WARRANTIES SPECIFIED IN THIS SECTION, PROVIDER MAKES NO WARRANTIES, EITHER EXPRESS OR IMPLIED, INCLUDING WITHOUT LIMITATION ANY IMPLIED WARRANTIES OF MERCHANTABILITY OR FITNESS FOR A PARTICULAR PURPOSE.

7. Indemnity

(a) *Indemnification.* Provider will indemnify, defend, and settle at its expense any third party claim, suit, or proceeding against Recipient claiming that the Software infringes intellectual property rights (collectively, the "Indemnified Claims"). Notwithstanding the foregoing, the following do not constitute Indemnified Claims: claims, suits, or proceedings arising out of (i) revisions to the Software made by Recipient without Provider's advanced written consent, or (ii) Recipient's failure to incorporate Software updates or upgrades that would have avoided the alleged infringement, provided Provider informed Recipient in writing that such updates could avoid infringement, and Provider made such updates available without additional compensation.

(b) *Litigation.* Recipient will give Provider prompt notice of, and Provider will control the defense of, any Indemnified Claim, including appeals, negotiations, and any settlement or compromise thereof; provided that Recipient will have the right to approve the terms of any settlement or compromise that restricts its rights granted under this Agreement or subjects it to any ongoing obligations.

8. Limitation of Liability

(a) *Limitations.* Except as provided below in Subsection 8(b): (i) IN NO EVENT WILL EITHER PARTY'S LIABILITY ARISING OUT OF OR RELATED TO THIS AGREEMENT EXCEED $_____; AND (ii) IN NO EVENT WILL EITHER PARTY BE LIABLE TO THE OTHER FOR ANY CONSEQUENTIAL, INDIRECT, SPECIAL, INCIDENTAL, OR PUNITIVE DAMAGES, REGARDLESS OF THE FORM OF ACTION, WHETHER IN CONTRACT, TORT, STRICT PRODUCT LIABILITY, OR OTHERWISE, EVEN IF ADVISED IN ADVANCE OF THE POSSIBILITY OF SUCH DAMAGES AND EVEN IF SUCH DAMAGES WERE FORESEEABLE. THE LIABILITIES LIMITED BY THIS SUBSECTION 8(a) INCLUDE, WITHOUT LIMITATION, LIABILITY FOR NEGLIGENCE.

(b) *Exclusions.* The provisions of Subsection 8(a) above do not apply to: (i) claims arising out of or related to breach of the warranty in Section 6(b); (ii) claims pursuant to Section 7; or (iii) claims for attorney's fees and other litigation costs either party becomes entitled to recover as a prevailing party in any action.

9. Confidentiality

(a) *Confidential Information.* "Confidential Information" refers to the following items one party to this Agreement (the "Discloser") discloses to the other party (the "Receiver"): (i) any document the Discloser marks "Confidential"; (ii) any information the Discloser orally designates as "Confidential" at the time of disclosure, provided the Discloser confirms such designation in writing within fifteen (15) Business Days; and (iii) any source code disclosed by Provider, including without limitation the Software's source code, whether or not marked as confidential. Notwithstanding the foregoing, Confidential Information does not include information that: (A) is in the Receiver's possession at the time of disclosure; (B) is independently developed by the Receiver without use of or reference to Confidential Information; (C) becomes known publicly, before or after disclosure, other than as a result of the Receiver's improper action or inaction; or (D) is approved for release in writing by the Discloser.

(b) *Nondisclosure.* The Receiver will not use the Confidential Information for any purpose other than to facilitate the provision of services required by Section 2 above (the "Purpose"). The Receiver will not: (i) disclose Confidential Information to any employee or contractor of the Receiver unless such person needs access in order to facilitate the Purpose and executes a nondisclosure agreement with the Receiver, with terms no less restrictive than those of this Section 9; or (ii) disclose any Confidential Information to any other third party without the Discloser's prior written consent. Without limiting the generality of the foregoing, the Receiver will protect the Confidential Information with the same degree of care that it uses to protect its own confidential information of similar nature and importance, but no less than reasonable care. The Receiver will notify the Discloser in writing of any misuse or misappropriation of Confidential Information that comes to the Receiver's attention. However, the Receiver may disclose Confidential Information as required by applicable law or by proper legal or governmental authority. In such case, the Receiver will give the Discloser advanced notice reasonably sufficient to allow the Discloser to seek a protective order or otherwise to contest such required disclosure, and will reasonably cooperate in such effort, at the Discloser's expense.

(c) *Injunction.* The Receiver agrees that breach of the provisions of this Section 9 might cause the Discloser irreparable injury, for which monetary relief would not provide adequate compensation, and that in addition to any other remedies available, the Discloser will be entitled to injunctive relief against such breach or threatened breach, without the necessity of proving actual damages.

(d) *Termination & Return.* The obligations of Subsection 9(b) above will terminate three (3) years after disclosure of the item of Confidential Information in question. Upon termination of this Agreement or upon the Discloser's written request, the Receiver will return all Confidential Information to the Discloser and certify, in writing, the destruction of any copies thereof.

10. Training

During the term of this Agreement, Provider will provide such training on use of the Software as Recipient may reasonably request, at the Facility, without additional charge. The parties will negotiate in good faith regarding the time(s) of such training.

11. Arbitration

Any claim arising out of or related to this Agreement will be submitted to binding, mandatory arbitration under the auspices of _____, in _____, with the parties sharing equally the costs of arbitration. The preceding sentence does not limit the right of either party to provisional or ancillary remedies from a court of competent jurisdiction before, after, or during the pendency of any arbitration, and the exercise of any such remedy does not waive either party's right to arbitration.

12. Notices

Any written notice required pursuant to this Agreement will be deemed received when delivered in person, by fax with written confirmation of receipt, or by certified mail return receipt requested, to the following addresses, or to such others as the parties may provide in writing:
For Provider: _____.
For Recipient: _____.

13. Term & Termination

(a) *Term.* The term of this Agreement ("Initial Term") will expire three (3) years from the Effective Date. Thereafter, Recipient may extend this Agreement for an additional one-year term ("Renewal Term"), one or more times, by written notice thirty (30) or more days before the end of the current term. After three (3) Renewal Terms, Provider may refuse additional extensions by written notice to Recipient.

(b) *Termination for Cause.* Either party may terminate this Agreement for material breach, by written notice. This Agreement will terminate thirty (30) days after receipt of such notice, unless the other party has first corrected the breach.

(c) *Termination for Convenience.* Recipient may terminate this Agreement for convenience upon ninety (90) days' advanced written notice. On the date of such termination, Recipient will pay Provider a termination fee of _____.

(d) *Survivorship.* The following provisions will survive termination of this Agreement, including without limitation the expiration of the term: (i) Sections 3, 6(b), 7, 8, 9, 11, 12, and 14; (ii) any obligation of Recipient to pay for Software used or services rendered before termination; and (iii) any other provision of this Agreement that must survive termination to fulfill its essential purpose.

14. Miscellaneous

(a) *Independent Contractors.* The parties are independent contractors and will so represent themselves in all regards. Neither party is the agent of the other and neither may bind the other in any way.

(b) *No Waiver.* Neither party will, by the lapse of time, be deemed to have waived any of its rights under this Agreement. No waiver of a breach of this Agreement will constitute a waiver of any prior or subsequent breach of this Agreement.

(c) *Force Majeure.* To the extent caused by *force majeure,* no delay, failure, or default in performance of any obligation by either party will constitute a breach of this Agreement.

(d) *Technology Export.* Recipient will not export the Software or otherwise remove it from the United States except in compliance with all applicable U.S. laws and regulations, including without limitation all regulations of the United States Departments of Commerce and Homeland Security.

(e) *Assignment & Successors.* Provider may not assign this Agreement or any of its rights or obligations hereunder without Recipient's express written consent, except to the extent that such assignment forms part of a merger or sale of all or substantially all Provider's assets. Except to the extent forbidden in the previous sentence, this Agreement will be binding upon and inure to the benefit of the respective successors and assigns of the parties.

(f) *Choice of Law & Jurisdiction.* This Agreement will be governed solely by the internal laws of the State of _____, without reference to: (i) such State's principles of conflicts of law; (ii) the 1980 United Nations Convention on Contracts for the International Sale of Goods; or (iii) other international laws. The parties consent to the personal and exclusive jurisdiction of the federal and state courts of _____, _____.

(g) *Severability.* In the event that any provision of this Agreement is held to be invalid, illegal, or unenforceable, such provision will be interpreted to fulfill its intended purpose to the maximum extent permitted by applicable law, and the remaining provisions will continue in full force and effect. To the extent permitted by applicable law, the parties hereby waive any provision of law that would render any clause of this Agreement prohibited or unenforceable in any respect.

(h) *Conflicts among Attachments.* In the event of any conflict between the terms of this main body of this Agreement and those of any attachment, the terms of this main body will govern.

(i) *Entire Agreement & Amendment.* This Agreement sets forth the entire agreement of the parties and supersedes all prior or contemporaneous writing, negotiations, and discussions with respect to the subject matter hereof. This Agreement may not be modified except in a written contract signed by both parties.

[signature block]
—*page break*—

Attachment A: Technical Specifications

[insert]
—*page break*—

Attachment B: Services Description

Part I: Customization & Integration Schedule & Milestones
[insert]
Part II: Maintenance & Support Tasks
[insert]

Index

978-0-595-40217-5
0-595-40217-8

Made in the USA
Lexington, KY
23 May 2010